The Wholeness Action Plan

Russelyn L. Williams

Copyright © 2018 Russelyn L. Williams

THE HOLY BIBLE, NEW INTERNATIONAL VERSION®, NIV® Copyright © 1973, 1978, 1984, 2011 by Biblica, Inc.® Used by permission. All rights reserved worldwide.

Scripture quotations marked (NLT) are taken from the Holy Bible, New Living Translation, copyright © 1996, 2004, 2007, 2013, 2015 by Tyndale House Foundation. Used by permission of Tyndale House Publishers, Inc., Carol Stream, Illinois 60188. All rights reserved.

Contents

Foreword i

Introduction 1

Chapter 1: Forgiveness & Our Perspective 5

Chapter 2: Forgiveness Begins the Healing Process 13

Chapter 3: Where Does Brokenness Come From? 21

Chapter 4: When it Appears That God has Let You Down ... 27

Chapter 5: A Different Perspective 37

Chapter 6: Thankfulness, The Next Step To Wholeness 43

Chapter 7: The Pressing Season 49

Chapter 8: Submission to Christ During Suffering 55

Chapter 9: Your Mind Will Need to Rest to Be Whole 59

Chapter 10: Case Studies From Brokenness To Wholeness & Rest ... 67

Chapter 11: Pursuing the Presence of the Lord 75

Chapter 12: Are You in a Healthy Relationship With Yourself? ... 81

Chapter 13: The Importance of Fasting & Prayer in Becoming Whole ... 91

Chapter 14: Walking With God 95

Chapter 15: Looking To Jesus 103

Chapter 16: Nuggets 111

Foreword

> "And be ye kind one to another, tenderhearted, forgiving one another, even as God for Christ's sake hath forgiven you."
> Ephesians 4:32

Faults are like headlights—you always see someone else's first. It's so easy for us to point the finger. Unfortunately, most of us forget that whether seen or unseen—you—me—we and I have issues. No one is perfect. "As it is written, There is none righteous, no, not one (Romans 3:10).

In God's master plan He keeps us eating and keeps stuff from eating us—now that's forgiveness.

Russelyn believes that 'Forgiveness is setting the prisoner free only to find out the prisoner is you or it's me.'

"*The Whole Action Plan*" is like the song penned and recorded by Tina Campbell after she discovered that her husband stepped out on her. "**Too Hard Not To**" is a sweet, yet powerful melody with a strong message and gentle plea to rise above the pains of life while encouraging us to walk each day as you live in the freedom and power of forgiveness.

Tina's heart is felt throughout the words as she reminds listeners that she's living the life she sings about. She quietly but loudly proclaims 'to not forgive' is much more difficult than it is to forgive. Like Tina's poignant song, I pray that Russelyn's book will allow hearts to be softened to God's will and true love worldwide.

When you truly love someone it causes you to let go—especially of offences. You will eventually see it's not always about having your way because it's not your life.

Throughout this book, Russelyn gives personal testimonies of God's steadfastness in protecting us and making certain we have all we need to live our best life. Each chapter is laden with key scripture references of the importance of waiting on God, forgiveness, trust in the Lord, and enduring His process. This book is about allowing our faith to be stretched by life circumstance so that we can become stronger, and be thrust into position to handle all that God has for us. The process of wholeness isn't easy, but it is worth it.

God's timing is the best time. So, in the meantime, live out your passion and purpose. Maximize each moment. Allow God's hand to develop you. Now is the time.

During my tenure at a former broadcasting company, I remember observing Russelyn during her Internship. She was smart, focused and eager to learn. Her walk with the Lord was obvious as she stood out among dozens of students and radio staff.

I'm sure waiting on God hasn't been easy for her, but Russelyn knows there is no life without Christ. She shares personal testimonies to remind you first hand that God is concerned about the smallest details of your life. God is interested in what matters to you. If He knows the amount of hair on your head, surely your secret thoughts, spoken and unspoken requests as well as your longing are equally important.

You have tremendous value and worth that isn't based on any amount of likes or followers on social media but rather God's love for you. During this process, he is preparing such an awesome life for you that even you cannot believe. God wants to do exceeding, abundantly, above all that we can ask or think.

When I think about my former Intern, lyrics to a beautiful song recorded by Shana Wilson entitled "Give Me You" comes to mind. 'Give me you, everything else can wait; Give me you (Lord) I hope I'm not too late.' Her message is loud and her mission is clear to all who will hear that 'you really are worth the wait.' I believe her ministry is to direct us to seek the heart of the Father. God's love is forever. He has the perfect life lined up for us with all of his promises that we will see in due season.

God's way is perfect. All the LORD's promises prove true. He is a shield for all who look to him for protection. - Psalms 18:30 (NLT)

I can truly say: Blessed is the reader of this book, which is not just for women only.

Effie Rolfe
Radio Programmer, Author, Consultant & Speaker
EDW Enterprises, Inc.

Introduction

Will You Show Up to be Whole?

One of the most important questions to ask a person who is broken is, "What do you want?" This question is especially important when the brokenness is caused by the person's own poor choices, such as putting up with a toxic relationship as if there is no other option.

The idea of thinking we only have one choice is all in the mind. How we think creates our reality, hence the scripture, so a man thinks in his heart, so is he (Proverbs 23:7).

This type of thinking points to greater issues in our heart, which create an inward brokenness that cannot be fixed outwardly by co-dependent relationships, situationships, or any of the things we use to medicate our brokenness. Our brokenness can only be healed by God and a conscious, consistent decision to renew our minds according to the His Word.

We have to cooperate with God as He does the inner work that will make us healthy and whole individuals again. This will allow us to make better decisions for ourselves; and out of that, be free to give and receive genuine love from others. When we are whole, we know how to say no and are okay with doing so. We don't modify our character just so we are accepted by others. Additionally, when we're whole, we are okay with being alone since we've learned to love who God has made us to be.

Brokenness can come in a number of ways: through our own doing, the doings of others, or life itself can simply throw us a hard ball. Although life may knock us down and attempt to break us, we can stand up and recover completely.

My question to you, the reader of this book, is this: Will you show up to be whole? Will you find yourself in God's waiting room, where He desires to renew your strength? Will you be there, waiting on Him?

I've found that, all too often, we humans desire for things to be within our control, and we could complete the action plan with a prideful attitude, thinking that we made ourselves whole. However, the truth is that only God can make us whole. We just have to be in alignment to receive it.

Peep the below scripture about waiting on the Lord.

"But they that wait upon the Lord shall renew their strength; they shall mount up with wings as eagles; they shall run, and not be weary; and they shall walk, and not faint." - Isaiah 40:31 (KJV)

Those who are waiting on the Lord in the above text had been weak, weary, and at the point of fainting. That sounds like symptoms of brokenness to me. However, their wholeness wasn't found in a 3-step program. Their wholeness was found in waiting, abiding, and depending upon the Lord.

When we're waiting on someone, we are dependent on that person. As long as we remain present, we know that eventually, our name will come up, and we'll have our turn for what we're waiting on.

For example, when we have a doctor's appointment, we show up at the specified time. We are present. We are intentional. We are doing what's necessary to be there, which includes filling out paperwork about family history, allergies, insurance, etc. We do what we need to apply ourselves, yet we aren't in control of when we'll be seen or when we'll get better.

Because we're present, we show up in faith. We wait, and we don't mind being dependent. It's the same way with God when it's time to become whole. We have to wait on the Lord, and when *He* is ready, if we're present, if we're willing to stay the course, if we're willing to abide with Him consistently, and if we're willing to depend on Him, He will renew our strength, making us whole.

This book is for those who are serious about wanting to be made whole. It's for those willing to do what's necessary. This book is for those who are tired of going through the same things over and over again and tired of their wrong thinking producing sub par lives. If you are, indeed, tired of the same things, read this book.

Wholeness, in many aspects, has a lot to do with submission. However, submission to the wrong things can break us even more. Submitting to the right things, such as to God, to His Word, to true worship, and obedience, even throughout discomfort and pain—

can bring a wholeness that allows us to endure, even through tribulations.

So, again, what do you want? Do you want to continue in cycles of bad relationships, attempting to become whole? Do you want to continue feeling desperate, to the point of losing your mind from all the drama of brokenness? Or would you like to be free to live and enjoy your life more abundantly?

The choice is yours. Will You Show Up to Be Made Whole?

Chapter 1

Forgiveness & Our Perspective

> "For the sun rises with scorching heat and withers the plant; its blossom falls and its beauty is destroyed. In the same way, the rich will fade away even while they go about their business."
> - James 1:11 (NIV)

The above scripture speaks of a natural circumstance that happens outside of our control. We cannot control the rising and setting of the sun that scorches the plant, causing it to dry out and fade away.

James is actually comparing how easily the plant fades away with how easily men fade away. It's akin to life unexpectedly throwing situations at us that are out of our control while we are rich and full of life unaware of what will become of us. One benefit of this type of circumstance is that it humbles us.

Additionally, it provides a clear perspective of how we should view things. Often during unforeseen circumstances, we draw conclusions and perspectives that reveal what's in our hearts. If our perspectives don't line up with God's word, then they begin to cripple us in our lives. This passage shows us that we need unforeseen circumstances in our lives to prep and catapult us to something better. Let's continue to read:

"Let the brother of low degree rejoice in that he is exalted: But the rich, in that he is made low: because as the flower of the grass he shall pass away."
- James 1:9-10 (KJV)

These scriptures tell us to expect circumstances that will humble us. As a matter of fact, it tells us to rejoice in them. Why should we rejoice when humbling situations occur? Because they serve a greater purpose; and that purpose is to move us forward and take us higher, not to destroy us.

It's important to understand this because so many people get caught up in their unforeseen circumstances, and they become stuck, give up, make things worse, or they even die due to the circumstance. God doesn't want us to die due to our circumstance. He wants us to grow, stretch, and move forward in life so that we are so whole, no one will be able to tell what we've been through unless we share it with them.

Tamar's Example of Perspective During an Unexpected Occurence

She was a beautiful young lady who held the admiration of a man who obsessed with the thought of being with her. His name was Amnon; her name was Tamar. Their father was King David. The two were half brother and sister with different mothers.

Amnon listened to ungodly counsel from a friend and devised a plan to rape his half sister. He succeeded at his plan. Tamar had a choice to make. Would she live her life in brokenness, or would she get past this, allowing it to make her stronger while claiming all she was entitled to as the king's daughter? At some point during her experience, Tamar lost her true identity and adapted to a lower one. This often happens when we're broken. We take on an identity different than what God has spoken concerning us.

Cultural Perspective:

Tamar, like all of the king's daughters who were virgins, wore a garment of many colors, signifying her virginity and indicating that she was ready to be wifed by an appropriate suitor.

Because of her involuntary loss of virginity, she ripped her garments away in despair. The Bible says she lived her remaining years desolate. She had come into agreement with the cultural belief that women who were no longer virgins deserved to be wifed.

Tamar's Perspective:

Tamar probably had so many emotions and thoughts running through her mind. Why didn't my father protect me? Why did he send me to my brother's house? Why did my father believe Amnon's story that he was sick and I was simply taking him soup? Why didn't my daddy see this and protect me? Am I not worthy of protection?

Her virginity was taken. However, she lived as though it was her fault and as if she had no recourse to heal from it. A woman who lost her virginity prior to marriage couldn't prove she was a virgin at the time of consummation; and thus, a husband could return her as damaged goods (See Deuteronomy 22:15-21). Tamar didn't want to risk that. She decided that she'd much rather play it safe and live a life sentence of isolation than take the risk of eventually becoming a wife.

Tamar accepted a sentence of brokenness for life. She chose to hide. She chose to live in shame. She chose to live in desolation. Why? Because the wrong perspective in her mind produced her reality.

> **"When we are broken, there are many wrong perspectives that come up in our minds which we must challenge with the Word of God."**

The situation was indeed hard, but not too hard for God. Case in point: Ruth had been married before. Thus, she wasn't a virgin; but she remarried the man Boaz. There is no account that Boaz shamed his wife Ruth for not being a virgin. Ruth had a choice after the loss of her first husband to live in desolation or to live in hope for her future. She lived in hope and the outcome of her future was much different than that of Tamar.

Ask yourself this question: Is there something I've experienced that I've refused to deal with and instead, I've chosen to live a life sentence, punishing myself because of what happened to me?

Have you ever asked God why He didn't protect you from a bad experience? Have you allowed a negative experience to cause you to fade away into isolation?

God's Perspective:

Our value doesn't change in God's eyes just because our circumstances do. Tamar was just as worthy of an appropriate suitor and the full life that Christ died for her to have after her horrifying experience, and so are we.

She was still the king's daughter, and nothing could negate that. I am sure several men would have loved to have had a chance to win her. It would be like becoming the son-in-law to former president Barack Obama. Are you serious? A chance to join the family of a king or former president? Who wouldn't want that opportunity? However, Tamar could not see this. Often, unforeseen circumstances that hit us out of the blue cause us to lose sight of who we truly are and what we're truly entitled to as children of the King.

I had an experience regarding something God had promised me. Everything seemed to be falling into place, but then things fell apart; and it hit me very hard because of my unhealthy mindset.

One night, I attended a class at church where the leaders had taught and ushered in the presence of the Lord strongly. I sang to the Lord as I walked to my car. When I finally got home, I went to the restroom, and it was there that God showed me a vision in my mind of myself laid out on my prayer mat. Expectant at the vision,

I grabbed my mat, and laid out as the Lord began to minister to me.

The experience I'd endured had changed my perspective. I no longer felt worthy of what God had promised me. Instead, I felt as though I had to accept whatever came my way. I felt broken and just not good enough.

During that time, God bought two parables to my mind: the parable of the Syrophoenician woman and the parable about the centurion commander.

The Syrophoenician woman:

She was a woman who wasn't a Jew, and the Jews didn't have dealings with the Syrophoenicians. God hadn't made a covenant with the Syrophoenicians, but with the Jews, Jesus was first sent to the Jewish people to reveal salvation, healing, and the Father. Later, He revealed the gospel to the Gentiles.

The story goes like this: The woman had a child who was vexed by a demon. She cried out for Jesus to heal her child. While the disciples attempted to convince Jesus to send her away, He continued talking with her, speaking in such a way that pulled faith from her. Jesus, who represents God, the Father in the flesh, loves faith.

He told the woman, "I was only sent to the lost sheep of the house of Israel." Jesus implied she was of lesser value in society, calling her a dog, which was how the Jews treated Syrophoenicians, but she wouldn't accept that identity. Her faith caused her to believe that she had an inheritance with this God, too; and she was right. Our inheritance with God comes through faith, not cultural affiliation. This is what qualified her to have her prayer answered. It is that message of faith that I believe Jesus wanted to communicate through this story. Jesus was so impressed that He told the woman that He had not seen such great faith among those who are supposed to have faith—the Jews. He then made the woman's child whole (Matthew 15:21-28).

We are made whole through faith, our ability to hold fast to what God said, even in the midst of seemingly contradictory circumstances.

God was telling me that if He fulfilled His promise to those who were not in covenant with Him because of their faith, how much more will He fulfill the promise He made me, His daughter? I could only cry in the presence of the Lord as I responded to God saying, "I did not know." I was so emotionally taxed during that period that I was not thinking altogether strait. It felt as though God had dropped me off to fend for myself in the world, but of course that was not true.

The Centurion:

The centurion's story is similar to the Syrophoenician's in that it was his faith that stood out to Jesus and made his servant whole. The story goes that Jesus entered into Capernaum and was approached by a centurion (a ranking soldier) who had a sick servant. Jesus asked the man if He should come to his house so He could heal the servant.

The centurion responds with great faith, telling Jesus there is no need to come to his home, He believed that Jesus needed to only speak the word and the servant would be healed.

Jesus' response was," Truly, I tell you, I have not found anyone in Israel with such great faith." He continued ,"Go! Let it be done just as you believed it would."

Again, Jesus was saying, If I did it for him, and he was outside of the covenant of Israel, how much more will I do it for you, and you are my daughter? Once again, God was pointing me to my faith, not to what I'd experienced.

Although Tamar gave up and felt her circumstance was too much, we have to remember that no situation is too far gone for us to recover from. It doesn't matter whether it was caused by someone else or ourselves, nothing is impossible with God. He promises to work in all things for our good if we love Him and are called according to His purpose.

To begin the healing process in her situation, Tamar would have needed to begin with forgiveness. She would've had to forgive her brother, Amnon, her father for not protecting her, and herself for believing she deserved a life sentence of pain.

Forgiveness is one of the hardest things to do. However, if we refuse to forgive, the offense will eat away at us, like a cancer. Refusing to forgive doesn't harm the other person; it harms us. We practice forgiveness so we can move on and free ourselves from the negative experience.

Chapter 2

Forgiveness Begins the Healing Process

Why do we punish ourselves when someone does us wrong? I know that sounds like an oxymoron, but it's true. We often punish ourselves when someone else does us wrong through choosing not to forgive. This is what Tamar did. She hurt herself more than anyone else when she chose to live a life of isolation because of what was done to her. Her life became a constant reminder of her negative experience instead of the freedom of forgiveness.

That's right, forgiveness brings freedom. The reality is that oftentimes, when we fail to forgive, we don't recognize it as a failure to forgive. Rather, we may think that time just needs to go by, and the feelings associated with unforgiveness will go away on their own, but the feelings will not completely go away until we actively forgive. Below are some points I covered in an article that provides insight into whether we may be living in unforgiveness or not.

The unforgiveness becomes an idol: When unforgiveness is an idol, we wake up in the morning and our first thoughts are about that person and what they did. Every morning, we wake up thinking about what the person did to us. We simply cannot get past it. We continue talking about the situation with others, trying to flush things out, instead of talking with the person who offended us so we can finally resolve it.

Our worship/intimacy with God becomes affected: There is a reason why the Bible says if we have an offense against our brother, to leave our gift at the altar, go speak with our brother, then come back to the Lord to offer our gift. It's because unforgiveness affects our worship, and it influences how far we'll go with giving our all to God. In a sense, we often give a portion of ourselves to the offense, seeking to figure it out, punish the other person, or protect ourselves from being hurt by this person again. Everything is centered around them instead of God. The unforgiveness has become an idol, and God doesn't like idols because not only do they hinder us from experiencing the fullness of who God is, they also keep us stuck.

We have a tormenting spirit concerning the person: We feel uncomfortable when we think of the person or when someone brings them up. We might even feel bothered when something good happens to the person. This means we have not forgiven them. The Bible clearly states in Matthew 18 that if we don't forgive others, God won't forgive us. Additionally, the way we deal with others is a direct reflection of how we prefer to have ourselves dealt with. That's why we are to love our neighbor as we love ourselves. Placing ourselves in the other person's position assists us in forgiving them because we want others to forgive us. We wouldn't want the world to stop simply because we made a mistake. We certainly would not want God to stop giving us chances. I believe that the tormenting spirit, as it relates to unforgiveness, is an indicator that something is wrong, and that something needs to be dealt with.

> "Then the angry king sent the man to prison to be tortured until he had paid his entire debt." - Matthew 18:34 (NIV)

Sometimes, forgiveness will require a conversation with the other person, especially when there's an opportunity for a relationship to be maintained such as in the case of family or close friends. However, forgiveness doesn't necessarily mean dealing with a person in the same way you did before. We don't want to set ourselves up for more hurt; we only want to see the situation resolved so that we can move on. It's okay to practice wisdom in setting boundaries and guarding our hearts.

I discovered the above about unforgiveness through my own personal experience. I had held unforgiveness against someone without realizing it. God, being concerned about me and being the good Father that He is, dropped a scripture in my spirit that I couldn't shake.

> "Confidence in an unfaithful man in time of trouble is like a broken tooth, and a foot out of joint." - Proverbs 25:19

Like the scripture, I had placed confidence in an unfaithful man who'd disappointed me. I had to take responsiblity for my part in the matter by placing my trust in someone who was unable to fulfill what was needed. It placed me in a position of having to forgive, and if that disappointment hadn't been dealt with, it would've continued to bring heartache to me, just like a broken tooth or a foot out of joint.

A foot out of joint indicates that something happened to knock that foot out of joint. When we see someone limping, we want to know the story behind it. We think, "What happened? Why is she limping?" It's the same thing with an offense or disappointment that has turned into unforgiveness. Pretty soon, others will be able to see that something happened to cause us to change.

Walking with a foot out of joint can cause a person not to walk out her full potential. It places an unnecessary strain on an individual and can cause even more damage. A broken tooth with exposed nerves creates greater sensitivity to hot and cold food and beverages. Similarly, a disappointment that has taken place with an individual causes an emotional sensitivity regarding the offending party. Isn't it interesting that the scripture would use these analogies to describe disappointment? Many cases of unforgiveness stem from disappointment; we wouldn't be offended if we were never disappointed.

The good news is that we don't have to stay in disappointment or unforgiveness. We don't have to allow our walk in life to become disabled nor allow our senses to become overly sensitive regarding certain people. We can choose to forgive so we can move on to wholeness concerning the person who has offended us.

Both forgiveness and unforgiveness affect our physical body; here is some research from

John Hokpins University:

> "There is an enormous physical burden to being hurt and disappointed," says Karen Swartz, M.D., director of the Mood Disorders Adult Consultation Clinic at The Johns Hopkins Hospital. Chronic anger puts you into a fight-or-flight mode, which results in numerous changes in heart rate, blood pressure and immune response. Those changes, then, increase the risk of depression, heart disease and diabetes, among other conditions. Forgiveness, however, calms stress levels, leading to improved health."[1]

On the contrary, the university also sites benefits for the body through practicing forgiveness. This includes forgiving one's self. Forgiveness produces the exact opposite effect of unforgiveness; it lowers blood pressure, plus the risk of heart attack, it reduces pain, depression, and anxiety; and it increases sleep and even helps with the aging process.

God knew what He was talking about when He commanded us to forgive. The command to forgive is God's love at work on our behalf. Forgiveness does more for the offended than anyone else.

---

[1] http://www.hopkinsmedicine.org/health/healthy_aging/healthy_connections/forgiveness-your-health-depends-on-it

Forgiveness can be as simple as beginning a conversation with someone who has offended us, or it can mean choosing not to talk about the offense any more. I have examples of both.

There was a brother I needed to forgive who'd played games with my emotions. I'd placed confidence in him, excited and thinking to myself that he was a real man of God. Ulimately, I was let down. I broke a personal rule of mine when he got a girlfriend. Normally, I don't call guys who are married or in a relationship unless I literally have to because I want to avoid the appearance of evil. Besides, my previous calls to the brother were ignored as if I didn't matter at all; so in a sense, I felt I was setting myself up for more rejection.

I ended up taking a different route, texting the brother. I asked him to call me when he got a chance so that we could discuss an offense according to the scripture below.

> "If your brother or sister sins, go and point out their fault, just between the two of you. If they listen to you, you have won them over. But if they will not listen, take one or two others along, so that 'every matter may be established by the testimony of two or three witnesses.' If they still refuse to listen, tell it to the church; and if they refuse to listen even to the church, treat them as you would a pagan or a tax collector."
> - Matthew 18:15-17 (NIV)

Well, glory be to God! This text message worked. I got a response and was able to resolve the issue and even come to a greater understanding instead of trying to figure out why things happened the way they did. I received clarity firsthand from the source, and

I was able to forgive. Thankfully, the brother was humble and genuine enough to communicate with me in resolving the offense.

Now, the conversation will not always go favorably, but even if it doesn't, at least an attempt was made to begin the healing process.

A second situation came up between another brother who just had bad people skills. He didn't know how to do certain things in an appropriate way, and it was offensive. I called my BFF to talk with her about it, and she felt my grievance. However, I felt the Holy Spirit was saying, "Don't talk about it any more." So, I told God I was done talking about it, and I forgave the offender without ever mentioning it to him.

There were times when I've seen the brother that the offense tried to come up, but I simply remembered what God told me, and left it alone. Now, it doesn't bother me at all. Allow the Holy Spirit to lead you in your endeavors with offense so that you can forgive and become whole.

Chapter 3

Where Does Brokenness Come From?

I believe brokenness comes from the fall of man, which was passed down from Adam. We actually see one of the first examples of brokenness with Adam's children, Cain and Able. Cain's poor choices came from his brokenness since he didn't feel accepted by God. The wrong perspective of feeling unaccepted by God, caused him to become jealous of his brother and to ulttimately murder him.

God responded to Cain, letting him know it wasn't an issue of acceptance, but correction. There was a correct way to make an offering to God and an incorrect way. God wanted him to do it the right way.

> *"If you do what is right, will you not be accepted? But if you do not do what is right, sin is crouching at your door; it desires to have you, but you must rule over it." - Genesis 4:7 (NIV)*

When we go back to the beginning, we see that Adam and Eve fell in the garden because instead of trusting and believing in what God said, they believed what the serpent said. Their perspective immediately changed.

When we don't listen to what God says over what Satan says; our perspective changes into one that causes brokenness.

They saw themselves naked and decided to cover themselves. This is a natural reaction when we become broken: We tend to cling to the nearest thing. If it's a relationship, for example, we cling to it, and in some cases, we hold on to unhealthy relationships, drugs, alcohol or bad habits.

As the bloodline of Adam continued, so did brokenness among his descendants. Let's look at Joseph and his brothers as an example. Joseph was faced with the temptation of becoming bitter and broken because he was put in adverse situations by his family. He, however, chose to cling to God instead of the temporary fixes that presented themselves.

Joseph and his brother, Benjamin, were born to Jacob and his first wife, Rachel. The rest of their brothers were born to Jacob's other wife, Leah. Rachel was the wife that Jacob truly loved, whereas Leah was forced upon him. Thus, Leah dealt with rejection from her husband. This same sentiment of rejection was passed down to her sons, and because of this, they felt rejected as well.

Because the brothers felt rejected by their father, they became jealous and competitive; they also had hate and even murderous spirits in their hearts that couldn't be fully manifested because God's hand was working in the midst of the brokenness.

The brothers initially planned to kill Joseph; but one brother, Reuben convinced the others, to throw Joseph into an empty well instead. Later, they decided to sell Joseph into slavery. Have you ever heard the saying, "Hurt people hurt people?" Well, broken people break other people or at least they try.

However, we have a choice of whether we'll accept the broken state. Joseph could have very well lived his life as a broken man. Here he was, a brother with dreams. He dreamed of being in a position of authority, but his situation at the time was less than optimistic concerning his aspirations.

Joseph had a choice to make. He could live his life broken, down and out and depressed, allowing himself to become stuck where he was; or he could keep moving, keep living, and keep trusting in the Lord to see what the end would bring. Because he made the choice to keep living, moving, and trusting, he consistently had to reject the wrong perspectives and decide to continuously honor God through it all, holding fast to the right perspective. This is one of the most pertinent ways to cure brokenness.

While brokenness has a way of immobilizing a person, that isn't God's will for us.

"The human spirit can endure in sickness, but a crushed spirit who can bear?" - Proverbs 18:14 (NIV)

The above scripture means that if a person is physically ill, they at least have their spirit to sustain them, providing hope that they will eventually become better if they endure and are taken care of.

However, when the spirit is broken, there are no additional mechanisms within us to sustain us.

Our spirit is like the cheerleader that encourages us to keep going, letting us know that things will be alright and that, it's going to get better. However, when the spirit is broken, there's none of that. There is only brokenness. There's nothing to inspire forward movement. This is why many become stuck in life, because their spirits have become broken, and they have settled into brokenness caused by their circumstances.

In order to not settle in our brokenness, we have to keep our connection to the Lord as strong as possible. This is what Joseph did. On many occasions, he thought and meditated upon the Lord while going through his ups and downs in life.

At one point, Joseph was presented the opportunity to commit a sexual indiscretion with his master's wife, but since he viewed it as a sin against God, he didn't partake in it. Initially, his refusal appeared to lead to a temporary demotion, but eventually, it led to more promotion.

God was with Joseph while he was sold into slavery and when he was imprisoned; He gave Joseph favor wherever he was. This is another thing that we have to be aware of in brokenness, and that is the fact that God is with us. Joseph knew that God was with him, and he acknowledged it.

"The Lord was with him; he showed him kindness and granted him favor in the eyes of the prison warden. So the warden put Joseph in charge of

all those held in the prison, and he was made responsible for all that was done there. The warden paid no attention to anything under Joseph's care, because the Lord was with Joseph and gave him success in whatever he did." - Genesis 39:21-23 (NIV)

"The Lord was with Joseph so that he prospered, and he lived in the house of his Egyptian master. When his master saw that the Lord was with him and that the Lord gave him success in everything he did, Joseph found favor in his eyes and became his attendant. Potiphar put him in charge of his household, and he entrusted to his care everything he owned." - Genesis 39:2-4 (NIV)

Just like God was with Joseph during his brokenness and trying times, He is also with us.

"For this is what the high and lofty One says, who inhabits eternity, whose name is Holy: "He lives in the height and in holiness, and also with the one who is of a contrite and humble spirit, to revive the spirit of the humble, and to revive the heart of the contrite. - Isaiah 57:15(KJV)

"The LORD is close to the brokenhearted and saves those who are crushed in spirit". - Psalms 34:18 (NIV)

God has a reserve of grace set aside for those who have a broken spirit, and He Himself ministers to those people. Thus, God gives them the strength to keep on moving to see what the end will be.

It was actually Joseph's consistent reliance upon the Lord, plus fear and obedience to His laws that allowed Joseph to be promoted each time the opportunity presented itself. If we push through bouts of brokenness relying upon the Lord, while remaining steadfast in believing in Him and His Word, we, too, will receive promotions in our lives. When we exchange our brokenness for trust in God, we give Him the opportunity to work in and through it. This is still true, even if we've messed up and made poor choices. No matter what, God has the ability to make us whole when we come to Him.

Like Joseph, God will not allow any of our brokenness to go to waste; He will use it for His glory and to our benefit because He loves us.

Chapter 4

When it Appears That God has Let You Down

I met a woman through a business situation who shared her story with me. She was approaching 40-years-old, and she'd been waiting on the Lord for a spouse. All of her friends were getting married and having babies, and she was the odd ball out. She became upset with God, telling herself, "If God does not give me a husband by 40, I will do this on my own."

God hadn't yet provided her a spouse despite her looking to Him and giving Him an ultimatum. She found herself a man, doing things her way. She ended up pregnant with her first child at 40 outside of marriage. Afterward, she was faced with a dilemma. Her boyfriend at the time asked her not to have the child, but she wanted to keep the child. He told her that if she kept the child, he would leave her and wouldn't participate in the child's life. The woman decided to have her baby anyway. She was overwhelmed since she received no help in taking care of the child, not even from her family.

Her family felt that she was grown at 40 and could handle the duties of single parenthood on her own. When her daughter grew a little older, she wanted to attend the daddy-daughter dance at school with her father, but she didn't know who her father was. Like her mom was believing God for a godly husband, and instead, she'd become broken and began to make poor choices; the woman's daughter was believing God for a father in time for the dance. Thus, the cycle of brokenness continued.

It had appeared that God had let the woman down. She'd been faithful to God, only to see those around her blessed while she appeared to suffer. I use the word 'appear' because an appearance is not necessarily the truth. Appearance has to do with perception and perspective. The Bible is clear that our perspective is not God's perspective, but His perspective is far above our own. Instead of giving into the temptation of doing things our own way when faced with brokenness, we should seek to get God's perspective on the matter.

"For my thoughts are not your thoughts, neither are your ways my ways, declares the Lord. As the heavens are higher than the earth, so are my ways higher than your ways and my thoughts than your thoughts." - Isaiah 55:9-10

When it appears that God has let us down, it feels like confusion. We ask why because to us, it just doesn't add up. If God is who He says He is, why are we required to go through so much pain, waiting, brokenness, and heartache? These are common questions that come to mind when going through hard circumstances where we feel disappointed in God. These are the same questions that Mary, Martha, and the towns people asked when Jesus was notified of his friend, Lazarus, being sick and close to death.

The Bible says that Jesus waited a couple more days until Lazarus actually died to go back to the town where Lazarus was. This shows how determined God is when it comes to accomplishing His purpose, which, in this case, was demonstrating His glory. After Jesus found out that Lazarus was dead, He told His disciples that it was time to go back. Before Jesus left, He told his disciples the purpose of His delay.

*"When he heard this, Jesus said, This sickness will not end in death. No, **it is for God's glory** so that God's Son may be glorified through it."*
- John 11:4

What's the big deal about God being glorified? First we know that the Lord is good, but the the big deal is that we don't know it as much as we claim to. Secondly, when God is glorified, He is made manifest to everyone to show He is who He says He is. Also, this manifestation of God's glory leads to more people being saved since they're becoming aware of Him. Remember, God's Word says it's not His will that any would be lost, but that all would come unto repentance. People won't turn to God if they don't know who He is.

God often uses us, His people, to reveal Himself to others and to us. This often looks like situations being or appearing dead, while God prepares a miracle for His glory. This is actually one of God's patterns. He used it with Abraham, the father of the faith, when He gave Him a child in old age. He used it with Esther, who saved her people. He also used it with Daniel and his friends. It's just a natural way that the Lord moves.

What purpose might God have in your life that allows you to walk through broken places that appear dead? Have you considered that God may be allowing you to go through brokenness for His glory? Remember, He doesn't cause the brokenness, but He uses it for His glory and for our benefit.

Thus, I conclude that when things look confusing and like God is delaying in answering us, it's simply because He is working.

Getting back to the story of Lazarus, the people were in a confused state. They questioned Jesus, asking, "Is this not the man who has healed the sick?" "Why could he not heal Lazarus?" All the while, they didn't know the entire situation was all a part of God's will to reveal His glory by raising the dead. That's why when Jesus spoke with Martha about her brother living again, He told her that He is the resurrection. However, she did not understand what He meant until the miracle happened.

Not only was God's purpose being fulfilled in Him getting the glory as One who could raise the dead, additionally, Mary and Martha also got a better view of who Jesus was. He was no longer simply the healing teacher but someone greater who embodied the resurrection of life.

Being determined to endure through brokenness gives us a greater revelation of Jesus and who He is to us.

We are to endure the broken places in life, meaning we're not to remain in them but to go through them to get to the miracle and revelation on the other side.

Many times, our pride will prevent us from being refined through the tough, broken areas in life. Instead of becoming humble, through it; we take matters into our own hands and cause more brokenness like the woman in the above story. She was so immensely broken when I met her, and I believe she was more broken in her disobedience than in her obedience.

Sometimes we forget that obedience to God doesn't mean that we won't have to suffer through anything. The Bible clearly states that those who live godly in Christ Jesus will suffer persecution. It goes on to say that it's better to suffer for doing what's right than for doing what's wrong (1 Peter 3:17). We have to decide to continue obeying God through the suffering.

When we remain determined to obey God through the suffering; it shows that our hearts weren't after getting things, avoiding pain, or living the easy life but that our hearts were after God Himself. A person who sets her heart after God will never be moved. She will never be defeated, because her hope is in the undefeated one.

When brokenness comes, it shows us what is in our hearts:

"Remember how the Lord your God led you all the way in the wilderness these forty years, to humble and test you in order to know what was in your heart, whether or not you would keep his commands. He humbled

you, causing you to hunger and then feeding you with manna, which neither you nor your ancestors had known, to teach you that man does not live on bread alone but on every word that comes from the mouth of the Lord." - Deuteronomy 8:2-3 (NIV)

The above passage of scripture actually points to a lesson that God brings to our attention when we need it; and that lesson is dependence on him. We see that God used the very thing that His people hungered for as a way to teach and train them to come to Him regularly. That's a little secret about the Lord. He will use the things that we want and need —but are outside of our control to attain — to teach us how to depend on Him consistently

What could God be using in your life, that you need or hunger for, to teach you to consistently come to Him?

This trains us to not just want God for what we can get but to establish a real and consistent relationship with Him. In the scenario in Deuteronomy 8, God is referring to when the children of Israel were in the wilderness and didn't have grocery stores or any place to get food. Therefore, God sent them food from heaven. He provided specific instructions, saying, in short, for the Israelites to gather just enough for the day because He would meet them daily. He went on to let them know that those who gathered just enough would always have enough, but those who gathered more, their food would rot.

As the Lord spoke, so it turned out. Those who gathered just enough, who trusted God to meet them each day and provide for them, had more than enough. Those who didn't trust the Lord, but decided to get it while the getting was good and then some, experienced spoiled food.

This leads to one of the next clues for this season where God is revealing what's in our hearts. He is also training us and teaching us to trust him more.

God wants us to know that yes, He wants to and will meet our needs no matter how bad it looks. However, just as important He wants to meet with us daily. The more we begin to meet with Him, the more secure we will become. When Jesus taught His disciples how to pray, He said, "Give us today our daily bread." Jesus Christ is the bread from heaven, and we need to commune with Him daily to simply be okay. With this way of thinking, we see that Jesus Christ is our greatest need.

Circumstances outside of our control also act as an indicator for both the pride and humility meters in our hearts. When there is pride, we'll go lower to be humbled; when there is humility, we'll go higher unto promotion.

For example, God knew that Job was a righteous man, and He bragged on him. However, Job's response in the middle of suffering showed Job something about himself that he may not have realized. He was shown as one who really did love God, to the point that he was willing to endure hardship. He remained obedient to God even through the suffering. This is a form of humility; Job submitted to God, even in the middle of his suffering. This is a sure sign that Job was due for a promotion. He was faced with the temptation to do it his own way when his wife told him to curse God and die, but he said no because he believed God. After Job's tribulations, he was promoted, receiving double what he had before.

Brokenness acts as an indicator to let us know whether we are strong or weak:

We're not failures if we're weak. We're just awesome candidates for the grace of God. The Lord has made a promise concerning this, stating that His grace is enough for our weaknesses. Often, our weaknesses are where the power of God will manifest in our lives. When we recognize our weaknesses, we should invite God's grace in by seeking to depend on Him fully in that area.

God will sometimes provide opportunities for us to give to others while we are going through. Then, he may release us:

This happened with Job when he had to pray for his friends; then the Lord gave him double:

"So now take seven bulls and seven rams and go to my servant Job and sacrifice a burnt offering for yourselves. My servant Job will pray for you, and I will accept his prayer and not deal with you according to your folly. You have not spoken the truth about me, as my servant Job has." So Eliphaz the Temanite, Bildad the Shuhite and Zophar the Naamathite did what the Lord told them; and the Lord accepted Job's prayer.

After Job had prayed for his friends, the Lord restored his fortunes and gave him twice as much as he had before." Job 42:8-10 (NIV)

Afterward, his friends and remaining family came and comforted him. God will also surround you with people who will restore, heal, and comfort you.

"All his brothers and sisters and everyone who had known him before came and ate with him in his house. They comforted and consoled him over all the trouble the Lord had brought on him, and each one gave him a piece of silver and a gold ring." - Job 42:11 (NIV)

Ultimately, Job was promoted. If we allow God to do his work in us and to shift our perspectives to His, we will be promoted as well.

Thankfully, the woman mentioned at the introduction of this chapter has been allowing the Lord to do great work in her life. She's learned how to trust God in new ways and is providing a great example to her daughter on trusting in God. Her new found hope in God models to her daughter that the cycle of brokenness can, indeed, be destroyed, and she'll see there is recovery after poor choices.

Someone has to stand up and stop the cycle of brokenness. Now, this doesn't mean that we'll never face brokenness, but it shouldn't become the norm for our lives. We have a choice. One of the things I love about Joseph is that he stopped the cycle of brokenness in his family.

On his deathbed, he told his descendants to carry his bones out of Egypt when God delivered them. He was giving them a word about the forthcoming brokenness they would face in Egypt. Yes, they would be in slavery, but God would eventually free them.

Joseph was teaching his descendants to always maintain hope in spite of the circumstances at hand. This is a very strong key in overcoming brokenness and walking into wholeness. We have to always maintain hope, no matter what's going on. We have to look beyond our circumstance to the future. We have to get a word from God to wage war for our future. This is what Joseph learned to do when he was coming of age, during his experience with brokenness.

Chapter 5

A Different Perspective

Those who feel that God has let them down will need a different perspective. They will need God's perspective. Take a few minutes and read Hebrews 6. It seems to allude to someone who has walked with God, had an expectation in God, but didn't see the expectation come to pass just yet, despite the work, faith, and believing that was placed in God.

Interestingly, the passage follows up by speaking about how land that drinks rain often produces a crop; then it talks about how the land that produces thorns and such will be burned.

These scriptural references put me in the mind of someone with an expectation of a harvest. It's interesting that it starts out talking about mature believers who've experienced Christ in depth and the possibility of them turning away from everything.

I genuinely believe that it's Satan's plan to cause us to dishonor our experiences with God when we're at the point of disappointment and brokenness. I believe Satan wants to use our seeming disappointment and brokenness to make us turn away from God altogether, as if He isn't the true hope.

The chapter also speaks a lot about expectation, which is something that's easy to lose when we're broken.

When we lose our expectation, we simply forget and lose hope for our future, even though we have tasted what is good in the past. In essence, this robs us of God's promise. Hence, the mentioning later in Hebrews 6 that through faith and patience, we inherit the promises of God.

The chapter goes on to say that even though our expectation may wane, and it feels like the words we've received from God and the work we've done in hopes of a harvest were in vain, He hasn't forgotten our works nor discounted them. Additionally, the chapter talks about God's justice in doing what's right:

> *"God is not unjust, he will not forget your work and the love you have shown him as you have helped his people and continue to help them. We want each of you to show this same diligence to the very end, so that what you hope for may be fully realized. We do not want you to become lazy, but to imitate those who through faith and patience inherit what has been promised." - Hebrews 6:10-12 (NIV)*

The truth of the matter is sometimes, after diligently laboring for the Lord and the expectation of what He's promised doesn't happen, we may not only lose our hope, but we might also become lazy in being obedient to the Lord and begin falling away.

This nearly happened to me, but by the grace of God, I'm still happily in the faith, and I'm thankful. During the last season of my life, I was so passionate about the things of God and loving people that I wrote a weekly blog, hosted quarterly encouragement groups, worked full-time, volunteered at church, used off days from work to teach on healthy relationships in public high schools, and hosted and produced a Christian radio show. I did all of this while seeking to maintain friendships and family relationships, plus keeping my own house in tact. Of course, these activities required meetings and additional functions that were mandatory to attend, and because I worked for a non-profit, I often found myself covering additional positions.

In short, I became tired and worn out. I was defintely approaching a season where I would have to rest or else I would have completly given out. To my disappointment, I'd become somewhat excited during my time of rest because I was getting prophetic words about a promise that God was preparing me for.

However, instead of that promise coming to past, a great deal of pain came into my world. I was already worn out; but I had to process the pain that had come into my life. If that wasn't enough, those who hadn't given their lives to the Lord as I had were blessed with what I was believing God for while I learned to suffer through my new found pain. It wasn't like I hadn't endured hardships before, because that's life at times, but this hit me like nothing else ever had before.

The experience produced questions and confusion in me. I could really see myself in the story of the prodigal son. God used this story to minister to me a lot during that season.

I recently found an interesting entry in my journal that I'd written when God was teaching me about son-ship:

"Servants work for an inheritance; sons receive it as a gift."

It wasn't that God was judging or punishing me as if I wasn't good enough for his promise; he was trying to promote the way I saw myself. He was allowing me to see that yes, He notices and appreciates the work I do for Him, but He doesn't want me to be confused, thinking that He only does for me because I've worked for Him. He wanted me to know that He genuinely loves me as His daughter—one who is in covenant with Him—and He has vowed to be responsible for me forever, simply because He loves me.

God wanted me to see that my worth didn't change just because of the good things I've done nor the bad things. This is the sum total of the prodigal son story. Both sons were worthy of the highest honor, which was complete acceptance as royal sons of the King, despite their track record with Him.

One son had a seemingly perfect track record, while the other was very unappreciative of his father's goodness; thus, he sqaundered what was given to him. When the righteous son saw the rebellious son being celebrated after his return, the righteous son was angry and refused to celebrate his brother.

He felt that his father was being unjust, the son reminded him that even though he'd stuck by him faithfully a fattened calf was never killed in his honor. His father reassured him, letting him know that everything he owned belonged to him also. He emphasized the need to celebrate the rebellious son, who'd recently come to his senses.

The son who strayed had an identity crisis, feeling as though he was no longer good enough to be a son because of his poor behavior. The faithful son had an identity crisis as well; he felt like he wasn't good enough to be celebrated like his brother. God's answer was not to change the circumstance, but to change the mindset.

> **God's answer was not to change the circumstance, but to change the mindset.**

When God, through the sons' father, ordered his servants to bring the golden staff and royal robe for the rebellious son, He was changing the way that son saw himself. When the father sat with the faithful son, patiently pleading with him, he was changing the way he saw himself. He wanted the faithful son to rest in what he already had.

The wrong perspective is a trap that makes us feel that God is unjust. I believe that many pastors, preachers, teachers, and ministers have experienced the feeling that God was being unfair to them. Many have gotten so angry with God, they gave up a life for Him altogether. However, the proper thing to do is get the right perspective then continue to the end in such a way where we inherit what we've been expecting all along and then some. I have a more detailed three-part series on the prodigal son on my blog, *"Intercession For A Generation"*, entitled *"Why Do the Rebellious Get Blessed While The Faithful Suffer? - Prodigal Parts 1, 2 and 3."*

Now that I've gone through the process of having my perspective changed, I'm thankful that God didn't bring His promise to pass right away. Had He given it to me right away, I probably would've been prideful and unthankful, thinking that it was because of all the work I'd done and the faithfulness I'd shown. However, I now understand that although my works are good, they would be nothing at all without God's grace. It's His grace that ultimately brings us to His promises. His grace also empowers us to receive salvation and to walk it out by faith, all the way to the end, and because of this, I am thankful.

Chapter 6

Thankfulness, The Next Step To Wholeness

Now, that your perspective has changed while your situation hasn't. Thankfulness will be one of the primary ways you maintain that right perspective. Maintaining the right attitude in life, regardless of the situation, will produce a beautiful character that teaches you how to operate no matter what comes your way. It also shows you how to trust God more, which, in essence, prepares you for more.

You'll be able to handle more by having the perspective of thankfulness. This is why the Bible says that godliness with contentment is great gain.

As God was making me whole, one of the things I did was pray that He would open up my eyes to His goodness. I believe that God does good things for us all the time; we just don't always recognize it. I wanted to start seeing it more often, and I knew I would need some help.

God started bringing things to my mind that I'd gone through as a kid that seemed impossible to get over at the time, yet I had. Part of my discomfort and pain came from God shifting things around in my life and digging up things in me that I didn't even know were there. He brought up painful things like wrong perspectives I had of myself and dependence on vices, such as fantasy lust, instead of Him.

It was funny because at one point, as he was shifting things in my world, I heard the Lord say, "Oh yeah, you don't need that crutch." It was really awesome of the Lord to let me in on what He was doing. It was clear who was in control and who was not. God was in control of everything going on, even though it felt like my world was upside down. All I had to do was trust Him; I literally had no other choice. God wasn't allowing me to depend on anything more than Him.

My crutches were things I leaned on more than Christ because I could touch, see, feel, or connect to them. So often, we hang on to our crutches, which are really idols, during times of brokenness as if it's the norm and unless God breaks up our world, we will continue on as if nothing is even wrong. Wholeness requires growth. It also requires discomfort, and that discomfort involves some pain, but if we learn to be thankful for what God is doing, we'll see that our pain is worth it.

What are some crutches in your personal life that God is delivering you from?

Are you thankful that you are no longer in the same place you were before God's deliverance process?

Since the Lord began the process of wholeness in me, I haven't struggled with some of the things I used to in former seasons. The development God was taking me through was really pruning me and making me better. I began to thank God for that. I even gave myself a personal rule of not allowing myself to complain. When I was tempted to do so, I would turn it into a praise. I would say things like, "I thank God this is not worse." I felt that if God could get me through this process, make me better, cause me to trust Him more, and sustain me, the least I could do was be thankful for it.

Besides, complaining only leaves us stuck, while thankfulness is an open runway for us to take flight. Just think about the children of Israel. While they were in the wilderness, God took them the long way because they weren't yet developed enough to defeat their enemies had they gone the shorter way. However, He sustained them during the long process. The scripture says they were in the wilderness for 40 years and their shoes nor their clothes wore out. They always had food for their bellies and direction from God. They had nothing to complain about since all of their needs were supplied., but because God did not do things the way they expected, they complained.

God was tempted to destroy them due to their griping and complaining. His judgment even fell on some of them, and many did not enter into their promised land. Again, complaining will leave you stuck, while thankfulness sets the runway for you to take flight.

I'm convinced that complaining is a manifestation of unbelief. Despite the many good things the Lord had done for the children of Israel, many complained, remaining in disbelief. and because of their doubt, they weren't allowed into the promised land.

Thankfulness keeps us focused on the things God has said, while complaining keeps us focused on our fears.

I've felt so strongly about being intentional in thankfulness that I began correcting those who crossed my path, who always complained. I'd tell them to watch what they said and I would try to help them turn their negative speaking into thanksgiving. I reminded them that things were still okay in spite of their current trial.

This was my new habit. Of course, it wasn't always easy. I was speaking against how I'd felt, what I'd seen or experienced, but isn't that the way we are supposed to live?

"For we walk by faith not by sight." - 2 Corinthians 5:7 (KJV)

Well, would you look at God? Teaching me to be thankful, and to speak gratefully when I don't necessarily feel that way actually shows me how to walk by faith. Faith is so huge. Without it, we cannot please God; with it, not only do we please Him, but nothing becomes impossible. Isn't it dope how God uses the opposition in our lives to build us up? We really should be thankful. I will say that I'm not perfect at this thankfulness thing, but I'm better. I pray this scripture in Psalms all the time: "It is common for the upright to thank and praise the Lord." Admittedly, I sometimes feel like I'm not thankful enough because it's supposed to be so common.

I don't just want to give God common praise, only when I can see things are going fairly easily. I want to give him thanksgiving and praise when life seems to be more challenging. That's when it really counts. That's when our faith is built the most.

Lauren Daigle has a song about trusting in the Lord during a hard time that I played over and over again. Some of the lyrics are below:

> *"Letting go of every single dream*
> *I lay each one down at Your feet*
> *Every moment of my wandering*
> *Never changes what You see*
> *I try to win this war*
> *I confess, my hands are weary, I need Your rest*
> *Mighty warrior, king of the fight*
> *No matter what I face You're by my side*
> *When You don't move the mountains*
> *I'm needing You to move*
> *When You don't part the waters*
> *I wish I could walk through*
> *When You don't give the answers*
> *As I cry out to You*
> *I will trust, I will trust, I will trust in You"*

These lyrics speak to the perspective that faith in God gives us. It's only at the point of total surrender and trust that we'll begin resting, despite our situation. The wandering and trying to figure things out — the how and why or why not—doesn't matter as much when we become thankful and learn to trust God more. Also, when you learn to be thankful in the middle of less than ideal circumstances, don't be surprised if people start judging you. They will do this because you're being positive in a negative situation. Carnal people assume that you have not been through anything because of your positive attitude, but it is a choice. Just because someone chooses to be positive doesn't mean they have not been through anything. People are weird like that.

Keep being thankful, and keep being positive because that mindset is elevating you above your current situation.

> "In every thing give thanks: for this is the will of God in Christ Jesus concerning you." - 1 Thessalonians 5:18 (KJV)

Chapter 7

The Pressing Season

I remember my brothers and I going to the doctor as small children to get our school physicals. We took turns, watching each other go through the process. The doctor had a small hammer he used to test the reflexes in our knees. He hit them with the little hammer, looked down our throats and in our ears, and brought out the needle for vaccinations.

All of this must have appeared to be very painful to my little brother, who'd watched us go through it. When his turn came, he fought, resisted, and had to be held down in order to go through the process.

At the time, my brother couldn't see that this was a necessary process preparing him to get to the next level. In school, you will not be promoted to the next grade without having the necessary physical showing you were the least at-risk for getting sick or making others sick.

In the same way, when circumstances occur in our lives that test our spiritual, mental, and emotional health, we focus more on the pain of the circumstance than the fact that the pain is temporary and necessary in preparing us to be at our optimal best for our next level. Like my little brother, we fight against it, and when we do this, the season of testing becomes even longer.

What if we decided to submit to God's process and trust in the Lord to do the necessary work in us? What if we trusted His Word that told us to think it not strange concerning the various trials that come to try us as though some strange thing has happened, but rejoice because the trying of our faith is working a good work in us? The trying of our faith is working patience, and we should allow patience to have its perfect work in us so that we would be perfect and complete not lacking in anything.

During my most recent season of testing, I began to really appreciate what Job says about the subject:

> *Though he slay me, yet will I trust in him: but I will maintain mine own ways before him. Job 13:15 (KJV)*

It often feels like a death during a season of many trials, tests, and temptations—one on top of the other. Even though Job may have felt he was experiencing a death, he made the choice to trust in the Lord. He decided to submit to the process, knowing that the process produced death in his fleshy members, but life unto the things of God.

God is killing those things inside of us that would prohibit us from walking out His will in our next season. He is killing pride, fear, doubt, unbelief, comparison, jealousy, envy, strife, and wrong thinking. Instead of allowing these things to stay, He's producing life in us. He is producing characteristics like humility, faith, speech in alignment with His word, confidence and security in Him, and a renewed mind.

We have to allow the Lord to do the work in us. When we are tempted to deny God or believe it isn't worth it to live for him because He allows trials in our lives; we have to maintain our integrity and obedience to God anyway, like Job. It may not make sense now, but as we continue to trust in God, it will ultimately make sense.

As we submit to God's process, we'll find ourselves in a greater place of rest and contentment. We'll no longer fight against the process, but fight to maintain our peace, rest, and contentment during the process, continually submitting to God.

What this looked like for me:

Everyone knows that I'm that single chick! One of the main things that has been outside of my control is getting a man to love me for me. God has chosen not to bring that to me just yet, but to allow me to be broken. I've been waiting while the Lord works in me to prepare me for that promise. I've had to learn to submit to it.

I will admit that it can look awkward being obedient to God and submitting in the middle of a trial. I had to block out everything in my life that made me feel discontented. I stopped following blogs that made an idol out of marriage and failed to address the contentment required in the season of singleness. I became more intentional about enjoying my life now, while God does His work in me.

I was determined to rest in the work that God was doing in me, knowing I would get to the expected end that God promised me. I had to understand His vision of what He was doing and where He was taking me, and hold on to that above all.

During a period of consecration, God gave me some scriptures:

Brethren, I count not myself to have apprehended; but this one thing I do, forgetting those things which are behind, and reaching forth unto those things which are before me, I press toward the mark for the prize of the high calling of God in Christ Jesus. - Philippians 3:13-14 (KJV)

At this time, God was affirming me and letting me know that He wanted me to take my eyes off of what was going on around me and the people I was comparing myself to and to place my eyes on Him and what He had to show me.

God's calling for me was greater than what I saw in others' lives. That call required me to press without allowing myself to be distracted. My mission to wholeness and enjoying life would be to rest in God's specific call for me.

According to Google, to press means "to move or cause to move into a position of contact with something by exerting continuous physical force." It also means "to apply pressure to something to flatten, shape, or smooth it, typically by ironing. A device for applying pressure to something in order to flatten or shape it or to extract juice or oil."

In the pressing season, we have to keep going. We have to keep moving. We have to continue allowing the Lord to shape us. The pressure that we feel in the pressing season is God shaping us. We have to push pass that depending on God more consistently, and seeking Him while allowing Him to do the necessary work within us.

Chapter 8

Submission to Christ During Suffering

> "Yet it pleased the Lord to bruise him; he hath put him to grief: when thou shalt make his soul an offering for sin, he shall see his seed, he shall prolong his days, and the pleasure of the Lord shall prosper in his hand. - Isaiah 53:10

Jesus was compelled to come down from His comfortable place in heaven to earth, humbling Himself as a man to save us. It was love and compassion that brought Jesus here. In his Word, He says He saw men as sheep without a shepherd, heading toward the slaughter. The Word also says that, "God so loved the world, that he gave his only begotten Son that whosoever believes in him should not perish, but have everlasting life (John 3:16)."

This plan , that Jesus Christ would die for the sins of the world, was set before the foundation of the world. Without Him shedding his blood, there would be no remission of sin. In other words, our sins would be forever held against us outside of Jesus Christ's sacrifice.

Jesus is our primary example for surrendering. He submitted to God, the Father, in His suffering, to the point of total dependence on God. Sure, He could have called a legion of angels and bowed out at any time, but His will was to please His father, and He wanted us to be saved, healed, and free as well.

Therefore, Jesus endured the jeering, the mockers taunting, "If you are truly the Son of God as you say; save yourself." He still humbled himself, all the way to submitting to death. When Jesus asked, "Father, Father, why have you forsaken me?," he was showing total dependence on God. He was saying to His Father, "I am submitting to your timing in raising me up. If you don't raise me up right now, I will continue this process, all the way to my death, and you will raise me up later." That is what happened.

Jesus knew who He was throughout the process. He knew He was God in the flesh.

"But made himself of no reputation, and took upon him the form of a servant, and was made in the likeness of men:" Philippians 2:10 (KJV)

Instead of making a reputation for himself, Jesus humbled himself to God's plan. This is the first thing we have to do in submission to God. We have to humble ourselves to His plan. We should know that while He will raise us up, the when and how is totally up to God. We simply trust in and depend on Him through the journey.

David, like Christ, went through something similar. When He was in trouble, those around him asked daily, "Where is your God? Won't your God come and deliver you?" David got to the point where he encouraged his soul, mind, will, and emotions, telling himself to hope in God. This is an example of dependence on Christ from a great king. Our worldly accomplishments, affiliations, and such don't matter when we rely on Jesus. We're in a position where only God can deliver us, and we are cool with that because we know He is trustworthy.

Jesus went through his process so we can partake in the benefit of His suffering. However, in order to do so, we have to suffer with Him.

> *If we suffer, we shall also reign with him: if we deny him, he also will deny us:" - 2 Timothy 2:12 (KJV)*

> *"And if children, then heirs; heirs of God, and joint-heirs with Christ; if so be that we suffer with him, that we may be also glorified together." - Romans 8:17 (KJV)*

Every one who follows Christ will have a cross to bear. There will be some suffering taking place, but in that, we're not to lose our expectation. We are to have an expectation of glory. That is God using what we're going through for His glory. We also ought to believe that we will reign. Doing this means to overcome in every way and to have authority over what seemed to suppress us, using it for promotion, not demotion.

> *All that will live godly in Christ Jesus shall suffer persecution. - 2 Timothy 3:12 (KJV)*

For I reckon that the sufferings of this present time are not worthy to be compared with the glory which shall be revealed in us. - Romans 8:18 (KJV)

Don't lose your hope while you're going through the process of suffering.

Chapter 9

Your Mind Will Need to Rest to Be Whole

> "Beloved, I wish above all things that thou would prosper and be in health, even as thy soul prospers." - 3 John 1:2 (KJV)

Health, in the above passage, represents wholeness.

Another definition from Google: "The state of being free from illness or injury. A person's mental or physical condition."

"1. To be sound, to be well, to be in good health.

2. Metaphorically

a. of Christians whose opinions are free from any mixture of error.

b. of one who keeps the graces and is strong."

Strong's Definition: "To have sound health, that is, be well (in body); figuratively to be incorrupt (true in doctrine): be in health, (be safe and) sound, (be) whole."

I think it's awesome that the scripture gives us a vital key to wholeness: being at rest within ourselves. That is, having peace within our inner man, and it radiating through to our outer man. It's also found in thinking and maintaining the right doctrine concerning our beliefs about ourselves in relation to what God's Word says. Being in our carnal minds, trying to rationalize things, robs us of our peace and wholeness. When we're resting in the mind of Christ we're at peace. Resting in the mind of Christ is simply resting in what God has said in his Word.

The scripture makes it clear that when we're whole in our soul which is the mind, will, and our emotions, we will move forward as our soul prospers.

This is why the enemy fights us so hard in our minds when we're broken. He wants us to stay in brokenness. The state we allow our mind to remain in will determine if we'll move forward in life and prosper in all that God has for us or if we'll remain stuck in wrong thinking and the false doctrine we've prescribed ourselves to bandage our brokenness.

Have you ever been through something bad and tried to disqualify yourself with negative thinking, wondering why it happened to you? Sometimes, trying to find an explanation and figure out why something happened leads to wrong thinking and false doctrine. This can cause us to see ourselves in the wrong light and be at war within ourselves about what God says about us versus what we say about ourselves because of our experience.

Then, we produce things like fear and anxiety instead of faith; pessimism instead of thankfulness and optimism; and criticalness instead of grace.

I'm writing this chapter after a period of rest from the warring thoughts I've had during my process of brokenness and healing. I've since replaced wrong thoughts with the word of God. However, I recently received a call from a college friend. She's been struggling with the idea of being almost 40 and still single.

She mentioned several doubts and how she's tried different methods to figure out why she's single. For example, she felt that if she dated more often, she would have a better chance of getting someone. So, she decided to just date more men without really talking to or getting a feel for them to avoid wasting time with someone not on the same page.

My reaction: It's her life and what she feels comfortable with. However, she wanted to turn the tables on me asking why I wasn't willing to just go out with any guy who approaches me among other questions to spark alarm. Mind you, I was abiding in a place of rest.

My friend asking me these questions was her way of getting me to agree with what she's doing. It was also a distraction from the enemy to take me out of a peaceful place into a place of worry that would've driven me to act out of desperation, dating men I know I'm not going anywhere with.

However, I'd already decided not to act in any way that didn't bring me peace. My friend; however, was clearly dating these men out of desperation. She felt that since she's getting older, she has to do something before her biological clock ticks out.

When I told her I was at rest and declaring some things regarding my future for the new year, her response was, "What if it does not happen? My reply: If it doesn't happen, I'll remain at rest and in peace, but my faith, at this point, will not allow me to entertain the idea that the things God promised me won't happen.

In short, the conversation was meant to tempt me to step out of my place of rest and, instead, become alarmed like I had to do something else, or things won't work out. I encouraged my friend with this scripture:

> "The blessing of the Lord makes rich and adds no sorrow with it.
> Proverbs 10:22" (KJV)

God kept giving me the scripture when I was struggling with why things turned out the way they did and why I always felt I had to try and make things happen with men instead of things just coming together.

This scripture was God's way of letting me know that the relationship for me will simply come together at the right time. I won't have to do any manipulating to make it happen. God doesn't need us to manipulate things to have what He's giving us. If that was the case, it wouldn't be a gift from the Lord.

I continued encouraging my friend to remember our lives should be led by the Word of God, not by our fears of the future.

"Man should not live by bread alone, but by every word that proceeds out of the mouth of God." - Matthew 4:4 (KJV)

My friend is growing in her understanding and has come a long way, but she's still a bit behind due to her not walking with the group of women God has provided for her. She has been bent on doing it her own way, which has opened the door for wrong thinking and a lack of rest. That's not God's will for us; He wants us to have peace and rest.

Stubbornness causes us to go through more and removes us from God's rest.

"Thou wilt keep him in perfect peace whose mind is stayed on thee: because he trusts in thee." - Isaiah 26:3 (KJV)

The above scripture is key. When we focus on God, what He's said, and His word, we open ourselves up for peace; and God's peace is the catalyst for rest in God. When we're broken, we're often tempted to place our focus on others—even those who've have hurt us. However, we can't have God's peace by concentrating on someone who hurt us.

Some of us revolve in unhealthy cycles, seeking the approval of the one who hurt us, instead of working to become whole and removing the toxic person from our lives. This behavior points to an insufficient viewpoint we have of ourselves that needs to be corrected by the lens of God's Word. No man can ever approve us the way God does.

It's necessary to focus on the Lord and his word. If we focus on those who hurt us, we'll continue making excuses and have the wrong perspective about why things turned out how they did, but if we block those individuals out, not being rude, but using discretion, we have a greater chance at healing. Remember, our soul has to heal inside for it to manifest on the outside. Then, God can finally move on our behalf. We will be so whole that we can handle whatever God has for us.

It's also important to remember that our thinking can actually change our reality. The Bible even says, "So a man thinks in his heart, so is he." This is why we're encouraged in Phillipians to think on things that are good, true, and of a good report. Studies show that the way a person thinks can change, alter, and even heal previously damaged parts of the brain. See "Switch on Your Brain" by (Dr. Caroline Leaf) for more details on what scientists have found.

Our words will follow what we're thinking, and we'll begin to eat the good fruit of what we're saying. The scripture says:

For as he thinks in his heart, so is he... - Proverbs 23:7(KJV)

"Death and life are in the power of the tongue: and they that love it shall eat the fruit thereof." - Proverbs 18:21(KJV)

"A man shall be satisfied with good by the fruit of his mouth: and the recompence of a man's hands shall be rendered unto him." - Proverbs 12:14 (KJV)

In the next chapter, we'll look at case studies in the scripture of those who rested in God and became whole. Hannah, in particular, rested after the Lord spoke through the priest, telling her, "What you have asked for, may the Lord grant it." She rested in that, and the Lord opened her womb.

T.D. Jakes spoke of the importance of rest during a Q & A at Pastor Tourè Roberts' church. He answered a question by saying that rest is necessary to handle the harvest. Without it, we wouldn't have the natural energy, or the mental and emotional capacity to manage our harvest.

That place of rest in God is essential. I encourage you to ask the Lord to teach you how to do so. Sometimes, when it comes to resting, we feel lazy because some of us are used to working on stuff all the time. However, there's a time for rest and a time for work. There's a time for harvest, and there's a time to prepare for the harvest; that often comes with resting in between the time we've sown the seed and when the harvest is ready.

I also encourage you to be thankful for where you are. The more grateful you are, the more you'll see God's perspective; and the more you see His perspective, the more you'll rest. Don't allow yourself to be distracted. Continue to press, moving forward despite opposition, and rest in God while you're progressing to wholeness in Christ.

Chapter 10

Case Studies From Brokenness To Wholeness & Rest

Learning from others who've overcome brokenness can allow us to see that we can, indeed, overcome brokenness too, especially, since these examples come from the Word of God. There is a reason these stories were included in the Word of God. It was to give us hope.

When we've experienced brokenness for a long time, it's tempting to become relaxed and complacent in brokenness; however, that's not God's will. He doesn't want us to think that brokenness is our fate in life.

God doesn't want us to feel that life is all about hardship. There will be good times and bad times, and we can get through each season by leaning in and drawing closer to Jesus Christ. Below are three cases from the Bible where people were broken for long periods of time. Each person endured through the hard times, learned how to rest, and ultimately became whole.

Woman With Issue of Blood: Luke 8:43-48

Endured

This woman had an issue with bleeding for 12 long years. She spent all she had on doctors, doing what she could to get well. However, none of it worked. She ended up sick and disappointed with all of her hopes, ideas, expectations, and money spent. The woman had to get to a place of rest and accept that her healing wouldn't happen in a conventional way. Instead, she had to strengthen her faith in Christ in order to be made whole.

Abiding in a place of rest while pressing

This woman was secure in the fact that things weren't going to work out the way it had for others. Rather, she would have to rest and press at the same time. Resting is what we do when we're settled and we've crossed our Ts and doted our Is. We now know that our only hope for relief will be Jesus Christ moving on our behalf. The woman in this study saw her circumstance as an opportunity to draw closer to Christ, so much so that she figured out how he could touch Jesus' garment.

You see, our circumstance is a test of whether we truly believe God's Word is true. When we are in the test, we are forced into a position to believe God will move on our behalf. This is what the woman with the issue of blood did. The circumstance was allowed in her life to pull the press out of her and to ultimately show the glory of God.

Determined, she moved through the crowd. She moved pass the distractions of others. Just think about it. Back then, a woman was considered unclean while she was menstruating. Now, imagine living then and having it for 12 years. She must have gotten stares and whispers, yet she blocked it out, resting in God's promises and pressing until she touched Jesus.

Some promises she may have meditated on:

"Bless the LORD, O my soul, and forget not all his benefits: Who forgiveth all thine iniquities; who healeth all thy diseases;" - Psalms 103:2-3 (KJV)

And the LORD will take away from thee all sickness, and will put none of the evil diseases of Egypt, which thou knowest, upon thee; but will lay them upon all them that hate thee." - Deuteronomy 7:15(KJV)

You see, to get into a position of rest, you have to have something solid to stand on. the Word of God is the most solid thing a believer has to stand on. The Bible is clear that we enter God's rest through faith. We know from scripture that faith comes by hearing, and hearing by the word of God. We must have His Word consistently before us and in us, meditating on it day and night, in order to enter God's rest, which allows us to press. It becomes the battering ram that will force open your next door.

Resting in God's Word becomes the battering ram that will force open your next door.

The woman becomes whole

She moved through the crowd and touched Jesus, and He immediately felt virtue, or power, leave Him. It got God's attention, because faith always gets His attention. Without faith, it's impossible to please God. There's a reward for those who seek Him diligently and for those who've learned to rest and press in God. That reward, in this woman's case, was wholeness; she was immediately healed. By going through this trial, she was able to tap into the process with God of lying down all of her trust in man for placing her total trust in Christ.

Hannah: 1 Samuel Chapter 1

Endured

It's said that Hannah endured barrenness for a long 19 years (jwa.org). During those years, her sister-wife, Peninnah, discouraged her by constantly throwing in her face that she was unable to give her husband children. This was believed to be a competitive act that Penninah participated in to gain their husband, Elkannah's favor, because she knew Hannah was the preferred wife.

In the scripture, Hannah is painted as one who was sorely grieved. Her situation was completely out of her control, because she couldn't make herself conceive. She could only endure the shame that came with being an infertile woman. Despite God's promise to have no woman in Israel barren, she had to suffer several long years, wondering why she had to go through such pain.

Abiding in a place of rest while pressing

Finally, like the woman with the issue of blood, Hannah had to rest. She had to realize that she couldn't be good enough or work hard enough to bring God's promise to pass on her own. She had to allow the pain to push her to a point of brokenness where she just didn't care anymore. She pressed past the suffering and past the embarrassment and harassment from Penninah.

Hannah decided to go up to Shiloh (which is Hebrew for "place of rest") with her husband, as she regularly did each year. Despite all that she'd experienced, she chose to rest in God's word and in His ability to fulfill His promise. She'd already been through the worst, so what more could happen? It was do or die. She would not die, but she would trust in the Lord until her promise was fulfilled. She would continue to press as she rested with the Lord.

Becoming whole

When Hannah got to Shiloh, she poured her soul out to the Lord so much that she was perceived as drunk. However, she no longer cared what men thought of her. It was do or die. Her faith was at an all time high. After pouring everything out, she rose in the morning with her family and worshipped the Lord. A sign we are at rest, is the ability to worship the Lord prior to our circumstances changing. After Hannah went home and layed with her husband, God remembered her, and she conceived a son, Samuel. She went on to have five children, three sons and two daughters.

Man at the pool of Bethesda: John 5:1-15

Endured

This man dealt with his illness for 38 years and ended up at a pool called Bethesda where other ill people had gathered. The Bible says that the impotent, blind, halt, and withered were there.

I'd like to delve a bit into the types of people who hung out at the pool, expecting to be healed. I feel these descriptions are some of what we exhibit during our process of going from brokenness to wholeness.

Impotent: In Greek, this means "weak, feeble, to be without strength, powerless. To be weak in means, need, poor. To be feeble, sick (Strong's Definition)." We often feel weak when we're in the process of brokenness. We feel like everything is completely out of our control, and we're made to depend on God for absolutely everything.

Blind: When we're broken, we're not able to see clearly. We experience ups and downs in our emotions, and we wonder why. There is a glaring lack of clarity that forces us to buckle down and seek the Lord in fasting and prayer as never before. If we don't do this, we won't have a clue what God is doing in our lives. Even with our increased consecration, there will still be things that are unclear to us. Yet, this vagueness causes us to trust in the Lord more. While we don't see or know how, we know that God's Word is true and His integrity is sure.

Halt: This refers to the feeling of being stuck. When a person is halted, he or she isn't moving anywhere. It appears that you aren't progressing, when in reality, this can be a place of great progression depending on our choice to place our faith in God.

Abiding in a place of rest while pressing

The sick man still came and lay at the pool despite all the previous times he'd tried. His consistent expectation of being healed was a form of faith which allowed him to rest.

Became whole

Jesus asked the man this question: "Will you be made whole?" The man, in essence said, "Yes, but every time I try to get into the pool, someone else steps out before me." Those who got into the pool first were healed. After 38 years of trying, it was pretty evident that the conventional way wouldn't work. This man's faith would have to be greater in order to access Jesus for a miracle. Fortunately, his miracle was standing before him when Christ asked the question, and His faith made him whole.

Also, the Bible notes that this man's healing took place on the **Sabbath day**. This is the day of rest. Rest precedes wholeness and God's promise in our lives.

> **Rest precedes wholeness and God's promise in our lives.**

We don't know how long we will go through, nor do we know how long it will take for God to complete the work he's begun in us. What we do know is that we have a choice in how we'll get through it. We can learn and grow through it, or we can become bitter and doubtful, extending our time in the wilderness. The decision is ours.

If we, like those in our examples, endure, rest in God through faith, and continue to press, we'll get to the other side. On the other side is wholeness and God's promise. Let God's Word consistently remind you of His promise for you to be whole. Block out those things that distract you and cause you to doubt.

Below are some scriptures you can meditate on for encouragement while you go through your process:

"For thus saith the high and lofty One that inhabits eternity, whose name is Holy; I dwell in the high and holy place, with him also that is of a contrite and humble spirit, to revive the spirit of the humble, and to revive the heart of the contrite ones." - Isaiah 57:15 (KJV)

"You turned my wailing into dancing; you removed my sackcloth and clothed me with joy." - Psalms 30:11 (KJV)

"To appoint unto them that mourn in Zion, to give unto them beauty for ashes, the oil of joy for mourning, the garment of praise for the spirit of heaviness; that they might be called trees of righteousness, the planting of the LORD, that he might be glorified." - Isaiah 61:3 (KJV)

"They that sow in tears shall reap in joy." - Psalms 126:5 (KJV)

Chapter 11

Pursuing the Presence of the Lord

Sometimes, when doing what we feel is right results in the unexpected, we become discouraged from seeking the Lord. King David is an example of this. Although he had a right idea, when it didn't turn out how he expected, he fell back from seeking the Lord.

The story happens just after David had been through many trials and tribulations, running from Saul, who sought to kill him. It seemed like everything was coming together for him. The people who believed he would be king stood with him until he took the throne. As a part of the celebration of his newly appointed status as king of Israel, David remembered the Lord by bringing the Ark of the Covenant up to Israel from Kiriath Jearim.

Along the way, the Ark slipped from the cart. A young man, Uzah, reached out to catch it; the Lord was displeased and killed him. David's response was anger and fear, and he said to himself, 'If the Lord is breaking out on us like this, perhaps we should not proceed with bringing the Ark of the Covenant back to Israel.' So, he left the Ark with a family, Obed-Edom.

The Ark of the Covenant represented the presence of the Lord and a place to meet with and inquire of Him. God blessed the house of Obed-Edom, as David watched and was forced to dig deeper, reconsidering his idea.

David had been left in a place of anger and was very fearful of God. He had to consider if seeking the presence of God was really worth it. He likely felt that if bad things happened when he sought the Lord's presence, doing so might not be the best idea.

How many of us have gotten discouraged from seeking God because things got worse instead of better? In David's case, a brother died, so he feared that if he continued, he could be putting his life, and the lives of others, at risk. Have you ever fallen back from seeking the Lord due to fearing death? Not physical death, per se, but death to your desires, or the way you expect God to do things?

When we die to our own expectations; we are elevated higher to God's expectations. Let's not forget the Word says: "He that loses his life for the kingdom of God's sake shall find it." In the process of becoming whole, it will sometimes require a brokenness, a death, but with that death, better will spring forth.

"Verily, verily, I say unto you, Except a corn of wheat fall into the ground and die, it abideth alone: but if it die, it bringeth forth much fruit..." - John 12:24 (KJV)

When God calls us to die, He's calling us to die to old ways of thinking that will hinder us in the next season. He wants us to let go of our pride and self-reliance.

Now, let's look at the revelation of the story of Uzzah and David bringing the Ark of the Covenant.

As David watched Obed-Edom get blessed for possesing the Ark, he wallowed in anger, fear, and confusion; it caused him to have to take a deeper look at why God killed Uzzah during the first attempt of bringing back the Ark.

Next, we see David setting specific parameters on how the second attempt will go. He says that none are to carry the Ark of God, but the Levites because the Lord had chosen them (1 Chronicles 15:2).

He went on to say that the reason God struck Uzzah was because it wasn't done in this manner the first time:

"For because ye did it not at the first, the LORD our God made a breach upon us, for that we sought him not after the due order." - 1 Chronicles 15:13

Interestingly, Uzzah's name means "strength." David and his men sought out a good thing in their own strength, not seeking God for His instructions on how to do things. Although it appeared they did the right thing, and the Bible says they went out with instruments, praising and singing to God, it's clear that He wasn't pleased.

God had given specific instructions on how to handle the Ark of the Covenant in Leviticus and Exodus:

- Levites were to handle Ark of the Covenant and temple/sacrifice related ministries.

- Temple/sacrificial ministries were to be handled with reverence, meaning respect for God and His way of doing things.

- Numbers 4:15 specifically warns of non-Levites touching any holy thing or else they would die. The Ark of the Covenant was to be carried on the shoulders of the Levites and not in a cart as Moses had been instructed. (1 Chronicles 15:15, Exodus 4:5, Numbers 4:5, 15)

The lesson here is that even though we may be attempting to do a good thing, it's imperative that we also seek the Lord. It's crucial that we study His word, which tells how to proceed so that we approach God how He wants, not according to our own terms. God cannot just accept anything from us; it has to be holy, set apart, and done in the way that's acceptable to Him. This is where submission and humility come into play. Even though, to us, it might appear that we're doing everything right, when God calls us to go higher and deeper in His way, we have to submit to the process He established.

The scripture tells us that David sought the wisdom of the elders and other believers, which is good, but not enough when we don't also seek God. There was a time in my life where I was confused and wondered if it was worth it to continue seeking the Lord and the things that pleased Him because doing so brought unexplainable pain in my life. It felt like my own personal death.

However, I'm so glad I decided to endure through the pain and that God didn't bless me with what I thought I wanted right away. I believed that after doing so much work for the Kingdom of God my promise would be waiting for me, but that just isn't how God does things.

If God had blessed me with a husband right after I did so much work, I would have thought I'd earned my husband. I would have believed that he came because of my strength and obedience instead of God's goodness, which would have produced a whole other animal in my life. Instead, the goodness of God allowed me to go through a process that ended with me becoming whole, ripe, and prepared for what He has for me. The process exposed the broken places in me that I didn't even know were there.

To my single sisters and brothers, God calls us to be whole before going into the marriage He's designed for us. This is His way of doing things; and when we sign up to do things God's way, we have to be willing to go through His prescribed process like David learned in the above passage. It's only through doing it God's way that we will have success.

Sometimes, the process of wholeness will look like confusion, which can show up as fear, anger, and frustration within us, but after additional digging and seeking God's presence, like David, we'll receive peace and His instruction on how to proceed His way.

Chapter 12

Are You in a Healthy Relationship With Yourself?

One of the ways we can be sure that we're whole is by being in a healthy relationship with ourselves. This means not putting ourselves down and choosing to love ourselves as Christ loves us, unconditionally in spite of our mistakes and shortcomings.

When we're in a healthy relationship with ourselves, we forgive ourselves, and we give ourselves the grace that we sometimes extend to others. We choose to practice self-control and patience with ourselves. We choose to endure all things because we're committed to loving us. See 1 Corinthians 13 and ask yourself if you love yourself in this way? If not, what will it take for you to begin treating yourself like you desire someone else to treat you?

Please know that others learn how to treat you based on how you treat yourself. Are you a person who has absolutely no boundaries and says yes to everything, even at the expense of your own wholeness and health?

Are you a person who can't stop serial dating long enough to learn to enjoy your own company, likes, dislikes, passions, and dreams? I once dated a guy who was 36-years-old and didn't know what he was passionate about. I came to find out he was a serial dater who didn't like being with himself.

Are you someone who speaks of having a vision for your life but never take the time to work toward it? Do you always place yourself last in your life? Are you a woman begging a man to love you, or vice versa? Even worse, are you paying a woman (or man) to love you?

We have to choose to believe that we're worthy of love, respect, and the best life we can live. After all, Christ came to give us an abundant life, so why shouldn't we believe we're worthy?

We have to choose to believe we're fearfully and wonderfully made and be firm in that belief. We have to choose to believe that we're enough and that God placed gifts and talents in us to edify the body of Christ and to bring believers to maturity across the world (as stated in Ephesians 4:8-12).

Additionally, people who love themselves cut those off who consistently dishonor who they are. Even Jesus did this in scripture; he moved on from the towns who devalued Him by refusing to repent despite His preaching and many miracles. Jesus warned them of a harsher judgment on judgment day. Then, He moved on to those who valued Him and what He offered (Read Matthew 11:16-28).

Do you even know who you are? We are seated with Jesus in heavenly places. This means that we are seated high above all that attempts to come against us. Because Jesus Christ was victorious, when we abide in him we will be victorious in all things.

There are men out there waiting for a young woman to forget who she is and to forget her value and worth so that they can take advantage of her. These men can see the brokenness and hurt all over a woman and many utilize it as an opportunity to take advantage of her. Never allow your worth to be determined by anyone other than Christ.

A common weakness among broken women is looking to a man to heal us or to ascribe the worth to us that we should already be ascribing to ourselves. A man who hasn't submitted to God has no standard to measure how we should be valued when we have not ascribed worth to ourselves. Ladies, you set the standard.

On the flip side, there are women seeking a man who doesn't know his value or worth. Their desire is to use the man to get whatever they can get, and in many cases, it's money. These women use insecure men until it's no longer beneficial for them. The insecure man goes along with it because he never learned to love and value himself outside of what he makes financially.

These unhealthy practices lead to a lot of brokenness in relationships. A single person's foundation has to be firm, stable, in order, and whole before a relationship with another person can be built. Furthermore, a whole person can't make a broken person whole; the individual has to choose it for themselves.

Having a healthy relationship with ourselves starts with having the right identity—the fact of being who or what a person or thing is. When we're born into Christ, we're a new creation. We grow, learn, and develop into this new identity, which comes from God alone. See the identity flowchart below:

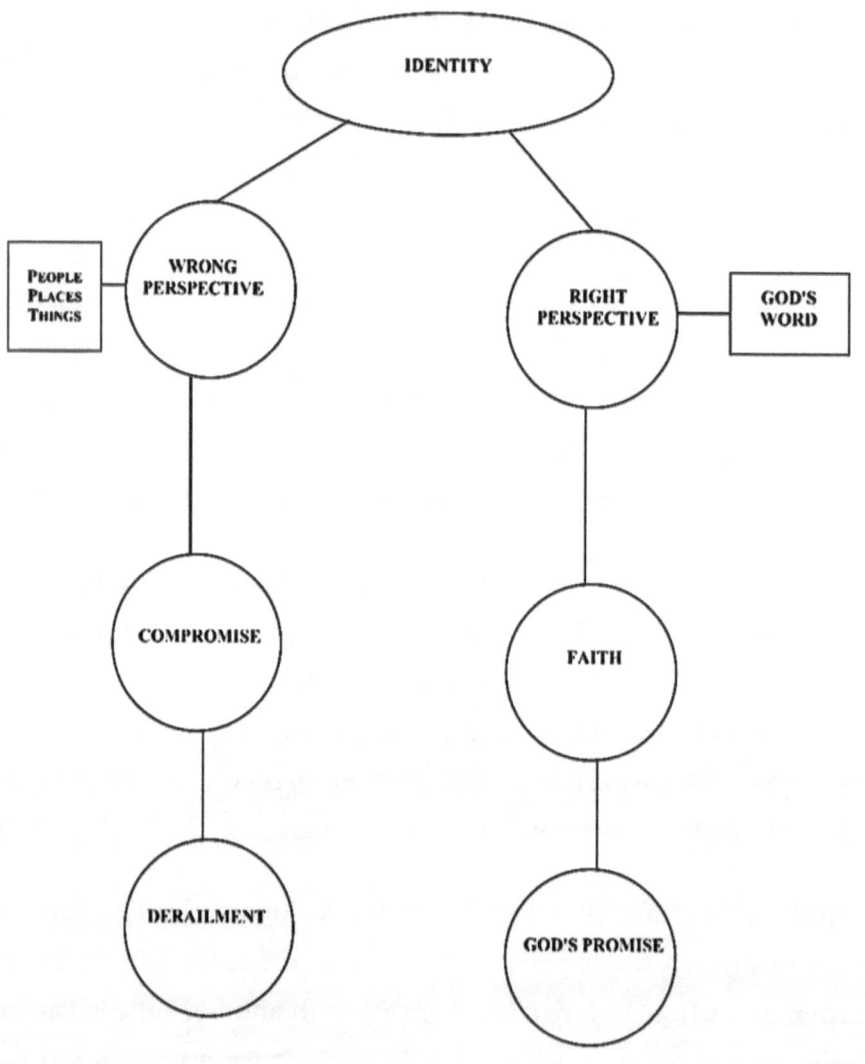

In short, the more time that we spend with God, praying, reading, listening to, and meditating on His word, the more we'll build our faith, and we'll experience the promises God has for us.

If, however, we spend time comparing ourselves to others, valuing others' opinion's above God , or drawing our worth from anything other than Him, we'll think wrong, act wrong, and get derailed. The choice is yours. Will you commit to loving yourself today?

Will you choose to make a commitment to building your faith in God to the point where you believe it, act on it, and declare what God has said from your mouth until you see it? This is the power whole people have in Christ when we move in line with God's Word and who He says we are.

Basic health tip

It is just as important to take care of our physical well being as it is our spiritual. One way to do that is getting regular physicals to monitor things in our body such as cholesterol levels, blood pressure, sugar, etc. In doing so, we can begin to make adjustments in our eating and physical activity habits. Starting these behaviors now, while we are young, will ensure longetivy of health to do the things we would like to do in life.

Joyce Meyer, said during a sermon that our bodies crave what we feed it. In other words, we can train ourselves to eat healthy. Once eating healthy becomes a habit; it becomes easier to accomplish.

Additional practices of the whole

Additionally, something else I do because I have a healthy relationship with myself is take myself out. Sometimes, I'll go downtown after church on a Sunday, or to a nice neighborhood, and just walk, eat lunch, grab some ice cream, shop, or explore new places.

Meetup.com is another option to get out there and develop ourselves socially. As people seeking to be whole, we have to be intentional about growing mentally, socially, emotionally, spiritually, and physically. Meeting and getting the perspectives of others helps sharpen us in those areas. We shouldn't be people who just go in and out of church; we need to connect with both the church and other individuals in more intimate settings to become better.

Recently, God has really strengthened my community. I used to be the primary one in my group who would call and check up on people or ask if prayer was needed. Now, I have people in my circle who check on me or correct me where I'm wrong.

Prior to this time, I was primarily pouring out. It is very dangerous to be one who pours out all the time without receiving it in return. Contrary to what some may think, hearing a sermon isn't enough. Sometimes, you'll need a hug, a "how are you doing?," or another warm gesture to be reminded that people care about you. People in healthy relationships with themselves don't allow themselves to be isolated.

We also need to invest in ourselves. One way we can do this physically is by learning about nutrition and working out. There are several blogs and Vlogs on the topics of health, nutrition, and exercise . A couple of books I would recommend on this topic are, "Let Food Be Your Medicine Cookbook," and "Let Food Be Your Medicine: Dietary Changes Proven to Prevent or Reverse Disease" by Don Colbert, MD. Fortunately, we don't have to search really hard for knowledge. If we're curious about a topic, we can simply Google it. Taking time to research can help you become a better you with hairstyle ideas, fashion tips, nutritional information, and so on.

As you continue to develop, others notice a more well-rounded version of you, and most of all, you'll notice as well and fall in love with yourself. It's not God's desire for us to hate who He made us to be; He wants us to love ourselves and see ourselves as worthy of love, just how He sees us.

In fact, God is actually more invested in how we see ourselves than we realize. I was listening to Joel Olsteen in the car recently, and he was sharing about the story of the Israelites when they came out of Egypt.

Olsteen mentioned how God required them to collect gold and precious jewelry from their neighbors. Because they'd been in slavery for so long, they continued to see themselves as slaves for many years even after leaving Egypt. It was all many of them knew. He went on to state that God wanted to give them a different perspective of themselves; He wanted the Israelites to see themselves as royalty.

This is not too far-fetched, seeing how God dealt with the prodigal son and his brother, who both had an identity crisis as sons of God. God is willing to go through great lengths to ensure we're seeing ourselves correctly because without the proper perspectives of ourselves, we won't be able to move forward into what God has for us.

The grace of God affords us the ability to be ourselves

Due to wrong perspectives we have during brokenness, we may end up with the harmful spirit of perfectionism. We might attempt to be perfect in order to be accepted by those who appear to be so already.

This is also where comparison and competition come in. A person who walks in a spirit of perfectionism is a person who doesn't understand God's grace over their lives. His grace, given to us through Jesus Christ, affords us the ability to simply be. We can be ourselves.

When we decide to just be, we don't have to worry about whether we're accepted or not because God still loves and accepts us for us. Check out Lisa Bevere's book, "Without Rival." It discusses how God loves us uniquely. There is no standard of being like our neighbor that makes us acceptable with God. God has given us our own unique blueprint and He expects us to walk in it. Through God's grace, we're given a seat at the table in the Kingdom of God. Through God's grace we're accepted even with our imperfections. God doesn't cast us off because we have flaws; he simply corrects them.

"All of us, then, who are mature should take such a view of things. And if on some point you think differently, that too God will make clear to you."
- Philippians 3:15 (NIV)

This keeps us from self-hate and being too hard on ourselves when we do fall short.

Chapter 13

The Importance of Fasting & Prayer in Becoming Whole

Have you ever felt far from God? Has there been a shift in your relationship with God, and you don't understand why? Maybe you've even questioned if God was hiding Himself. Well, the Lord could be hiding himself. I heard a well-known evangelist, Benny Hinn, say that the Lord hides himself when it's time for us to go deeper in seeking Him so we can find Him.

"Truly you are a God who has been hiding himself, the God and Savior of Israel." - Isaiah 45:15 (NIV)

All too often, God's hiding confuses us. We may think He has left us, but He actually wants to draw nearer to us. It's like an invitation to come higher; and one way to do this is through fasting. In the Bible, Jesus was asked why many Jews fasted often, while his disciples hardly fasted at all.

He responded, saying that as long as the bridegroom is with the bridal party, there's no reason to fast, but when the bridegroom is no longer with the bridal party, there is a reason. Jesus was dropping a clue letting us know what to do when we feel confused, spent, and separated from God. During this time, we must fast and pray.

Fasting is a type of mourning where one says, 'I'm not going to eat until I can get to God.' It shows the seriousness about seeking God. Additionally, fasting brings clarity to our situations, and it makes us more sensitive to the Lord's voice.

Jesus was suggesting that we fast, not out of religion or tradition, but out of an earnest desire for God.

During my season of brokenness, I fasted a whole lot. In addition, I began fasting regularly, on top of more lengthy fasts. However, when I got to the point where I felt I was doing it out of tradition, I stopped. I realized I was no longer fasting to seek and revere the Lord, so stopping was a way for me to guard the sobriety of fasting.

There's a good chance that the Jews who questioned Jesus were fasting for traditional reasons, or they were being self-righteous. Self-righteousness is not of God, nor is it genuine. It's a way to lift one's-self up while putting another down; it's like saying, 'I can do this, and you can't, so you're lower than me.' Self-righteousness can be something that broken and insecure people hold on to as a false sense of security.

However, when we fast and pray, seeking the Lord out of an earnest need for Him, we instead learn to depend on God. Fasting and prayer humbles and teaches us not to lift up or heal ourselves, but to be lifted up and healed by God.

Genuine fasting positions us to be rewarded by the Lord. In His Word, God says He's a rewarder of those who diligently seek after Him, and fasting is a way to do so. This practice also quiets our spirit so we can more easily recognize God's perspective.

A word of caution: There are some medical conditions that will prohibit certain types of fasts. If there are any concerns, consult your doctor. Fasts typically last one day, three days, five days, 7 days, 12 hours, or 21 days. Some fasts are done without food or water, and some include only water or liquids. The types of fasts can be combined as well. For example, in 2017, I participated in a 21-day vegan fast where I also took one day out of the week for a complete fast.

Additionally, when we fast, we shouldn't listen to secular music (when the option is within our control), and we should limit television. If you do watch, it should be Christian programming. We want to intentionally focus our spirits and minds on God and His Word.

When I was experiencing brokenness, fasting and prayer provided some of the most valuable relief, I was able to experience the presence of the Lord and write down what God gave me in my journal or in my phone's writing app. The benefits I received during fasting and prayer sustained me through the rest of my broken season.

It worked so well that I started enjoying fasting and praying a lot more, and it became a natural process. Sometimes, God uses our brokenness so we'll become consistent in seeking Him at the level that will be required for our next season.

God has left us so many tools that we can't be defeated; fasting and prayer is one of them.

Chapter 14

Walking With God

Although this book is primarily for Christians, I don't want to assume that everyone reading this is already saved. It's important to know that walking with God is the primary factor in wholeness. We cannot do so without being born again.

This simply means putting off our old way of living for Christ's way. We first have to believe that Jesus is the Son of God, who died to pay the penalty for the sins of the world, and rose again.

To be born again, one will have to confess with his mouth, and believe in his heart that Jesus died and rose again (Romans 10:9-14). Afterward, that person needs to continue cultivating his or her relationship with God through prayer, reading the Bible, and learning within the company of believers. Having a church home that teaches the Word of God allows us to learn and grow. The more we develop our relationship with the Lord, the more discernment we'll have when it comes to determining if a church is teaching God's word or not.

Not only did Jesus die for us, but scripturally, He's referred to as the second Adam, which means man. Jesus Christ was God in the flesh, and He humbled Himself as a man to redo what the first Adam should've done, which is to walk in his dominion and authority on earth as a man.

Whatever comes against us, trying to break us down, we have authority over it in Christ. In the first Adam, man was given authority over everything. Man relinquished that authority in the garden by giving in to the deception of the serpent. Confusion and chaos entered; however, we gain our authority back with Christ Jesus and are now seated with Him in heavenly places, far above all principalities.

> *"And God raised us up with Christ and seated us with him in the heavenly realms in Christ Jesus," - Ephesians 2:6 (NIV)*

Receiving the Holy Spirit

After we become born again, we can ask God to give us His Holy Spirit, the third person of the Godhead. The God head consists of God, the Father, God, the Son, and God, the Holy Spirit.

The Holy Spirit keeps, leads, and guides us and is responsibile for leading and guiding us into all truth.

> *But when he, the Spirit of truth, comes, he will guide you into all truth. He will not speak on his own; he will speak only what he hears, and he will tell you what is yet to come." - John 16:13. (NIV)*

Jesus did the same thing when He was on Earth; He only spoke the words God, the Father, gave Him. The Father gives instructions and Jesus Christ, along with the Holy Spirit, carry it out. The Holy Spirit is like our deposit on Earth, guaranteeing there's more of God to come. The Bible describes the Holy Spirit as our seal, or proof, that we've been purchased by God:

In whom ye also trusted, after that you heard the word of truth, the gospel of your salvation: in whom also after that you believed, you were sealed with that Holy Spirit of promise, - Ephesians 1:13 (KJV)

The Holy Spirit is so awesome because He is with us as we go through every trial and tribulation. He ensures that we get through them safely. Scripturally, He is known as the Spirit of Truth and our Comforter. Additionally, one of the Greek words for the Holy Spirit is parakletos, which means "to walk alongside of or to be an advocate for. We cannot lose with the way God has set things up for us to win. One of my late pastors, Dr. Angie Ray, used to say that "we were born to win." When we become genuinely born again, we become born or setup to win. I remember one of my mentors prophesying to me these words, "I can see you walking and there are pits set up for you to fall in, but I seen the Holy Spirit going before you, and He was covering each of them up." This has been my testimony, and this is how walking with the Holy Spirit is. We don't have to fall into pitfalls that others fall into because the Lord through his Spirit covers us by leading us the right way.

The Holy Spirit also:

- Warns us of the future and things to come. (John 16:13)

- Convicts us of sin. (John 16:8)

- Searches the deep things of God and reveals them to us at will. (1 Corinthians 2:10)

- Teaches and reminds us of God's word. (John 14:26)

To learn more, Google scriptures on the Holy Spirit.

"If you then, being evil, know how to give good gifts unto your children: how much more will your heavenly Father give the Holy Spirit to them that ask him?" - Luke 11:13 (KJV)

Many times, I've experienced the Holy Spirit leading, guiding, correcting, and directing me, whether He inspired someone to speak to me or He's spoken to me directly in my spirit.

During a season of brokenness in my life, I was at work, meeting with a client who goes to my current church. I didn't know her at the time, but she spoke to me concerning two big issues going on in my life.

One was me fighting for my self-worth. The standard that God set for me was too high to others, so people judged me and put me down. I had to fight to see myself how God saw me in spite of people's opinions, even those who I thought should've been protecting me.

The woman told me, "It is not that there's something wrong with you, but God made you in such a way where He does not want you to put up with certain things. Now, the enemy is going to try to get you to have sex outside of marriage."

She was addressing the fact that I was talking to a guy who was saved, in the sense of having said the sinner's prayer. He went to church—a dead church might I add—but he didn't have an intimate relationship with God. He was on the outer court, so to speak. Due to how I'd struggled with my worth, based on life situations and such, I was trying to make things work anyway. I also struggled with the idea that this might be the best God had for me.

However, His voice on the matter let me know that there's nothing wrong with waiting for someone who's on the same page as me. It's okay for me to wait for a man who has an intimate relationship with God and understands his role as a man of God.

There's nothing wrong with me waiting for someone who won't try to get me comfortable with sex outside of marriage, pretending that he will wait too, when, in reality, he plans to slip and dip in the cookie jar prior to marriage. That was the intention of the man I was seeing, which is why he and I had to break up.

The second issue the woman spoke of concerned my family. My immediate family was facing some issues I thought had been resolved long ago: domestic violence, mental illness, and the separation and confusion that those issues caused.

The prophet shared that there'd been some things going on with my parents, and God was going to straighten it out. She said, "You'll see. Everything is going to be alright." That, of course, gave me such relief.

God had even spoken to one of my prayer partners in California, who I don't speak to often. She called me, saying she'd had a dream and was praying for me. The Lord let her know something was going on with me. She was able to encourage me because she'd been through some similar things.

God gave me visions and spoke to me in dreams concerning my future as well.

Once, I was on the phone with an elder from my church because I had become depressed due to things going on in my life. On the call, God showed me a vision of myself dancing. He was saying that I would dance on the other side of this. This vision was confirmed with the scripture below:

> *"You have turned my mourning into joyful dancing. You have taken away my clothes of mourning and clothed me with joy"- Psalms 30:11 (NLT)*

Remember, the Holy Spirit won't speak anything that contradicts the Word of God. It will always be in alignment. This is why we have to know God's Word. If we don't, we'll lack the discernment to hear and understand God's voice.

While God does reveal things to us, He won't show us everything; He'll show us what we need to keep us going. Many of us want to know everything, but if we did, we wouldn't trust or depend on

God. Instead, we'd rely on our own knowledge. Because God is constantly calling us higher, we have to get comfortable with not knowing everything, and trust, lean, and depend on God.

The prophet, Elijah, had to be comfortable with the discomfort of not knowing everything. He had to learn to lean on God and walk by faith.

During a famine in the land, God instructed him to go to a brook, and there, a bird would bring him food for nourishment, while the brook would provide water. After the brook dried up, God sent Elijah to a widowed woman's house where she fed him, which was a miracle in itself. The woman used the last of her flour and oil to make cakes that sustained her and Elijah.

After this, Elijah performed a miracle, showing who God was to the govermental leaders of his day, Ahab and Jezebel (See 1 Kings 18). Later, he raised a widow's son from the dead. Had Elijah not learned to depend on God by trusting Him with the unknown, he wouldn't have been able to do the things he did.

Elijah had to be in the place where he moved in faith. When God wants us to get comfortable with the discomfort of not knowing everything, He's requiring us to live in a place of faith because He wants to use us to do the miraculous. When we allow Him to do this, we reveal His glory to others, and many believe because of it and become saved.

The secret to contentment:

Paul spoke about a secret to contentment in the passage below:

*"Not that I speak in respect of want; for I have learned, in whatever state I am, therewith to be content. I know both how to be abased, and I know how to abound: every where and in all things I am instructed both to be full and to be hungry, both to abound and to suffer need. **I can do all things through Christ which strengthens me.**"* - Philippians 4:11-13 (KJV)

The secret to contentment is dependence on Christ.

The secret is looking to Him for strength in times where lack seemingly appears and in times of fullness. It's trusting Him and His plan when we can see what He's doing and when we can't see. The secret to contentment is allowing ourselves to get comfortable with living in the discomfort of not knowing, while trusting that everything will work together for our good on a greater scale than we could ever imagine. Just look at how God used Elijah and Apostle Paul. Hmmm... I wonder what God has for you on your journey to wholeness as you trust and rely on Him?

Chapter 15

Looking To Jesus

This is probably the most important chapter because for the believer, brokenness should bring us back to who we are in Christ. Jesus Christ—our Head, God, example, Savior and Lord, allowed Himself to be broken. He was God in the flesh, and His purpose was to reveal God, the Father, to a dying world. In order to do so, even God had to lower Himself in the form of a man, Jesus Christ.

Brokenness lowers, or humbles, us. However, God uses humility to promote us.

Humility precedes promotion

Jesus Christ calls himself the last Adam. (1 Corinthians 15:45, Romans 5:12-21) Jesus came to correct what went wrong under the first Adam. The first Adam was given dominion over everything, representing God on Earth. Both He and Eve were made in God's image. However, Adam began going his own way instead of being obedient to God. He acted outside of and around God's commandment. Thus, Adam's descendants did the same thing.

Jesus became the second and last Adam and set the precedence on how we should represent God on Earth. Jesus was one who did not come to operate out of his own will, but he came to operate under God, the Father's will. He did nothing outside of what he saw the Father do.

"Then answered Jesus and said unto them, Verily, verily, I say unto you, The Son can do nothing of himself, but what he sees the Father do: for what things soever he doeth, these also doeth the Son likewise." - John 5:19 (KJV)

Living this type of a lifestyle requires humility. Jesus even said that He didn't come to be served but to serve. He washed his disciples feet, one of the lowliest jobs during that time, but Jesus didn't mind because He was operating in God's purpose for his life and providing an example of how we should treat one another in Christ.

Jesus requires us, as believers, to live a life of humility, and brokenness will always bring us back to that place. Looking at Jesus, we become whole, our perspectives are aligned, and we live in purpose again.

I can really appreciate being humbled because I can struggle with pride at times. However, I've learned to be thankful for the times that bring me low because it causes me to depend on Christ the way Christ depended on God.

Jesus showed that it would be hard at times but that it would be worth it:

Even Jesus asked for the cup of dying on the cross to pass from him if it is possible in anyway. Yet, in the end, He submitted to God's will. It wasn't easy for Him; as a matter of fact, it was difficult, but he proceeded anyway.

Sometimes, we're so excited about something God has shown us to do, and we leap out in faith and passion, but when the challenges come, we second guess ourselves, wondering if we can actually do it and if we are strong or wise enough. However, when we continue to move forward in faith, like Jesus, the grace of God will empower us to do what we thought we couldn't.

When it got hard to carry the cross, even Jesus dropped it a couple of times and needed help carrying it.

When I was going through, I decided to take a trip out to "The Shrine of Jesus Christ" in St. John, Indiana, which is like a museum with replicas of Jesus, the crucifixion, and such. I needed more focus on Jesus, and as I walked through there praising God, I knew I wasn't alone. While there, I also realized that even Jesus got overwhelmed and tired from carrying the cross and required help.

"And as they led him away, they laid hold upon one Simon, a Cyrenian, coming out of the country, and on him they laid the cross, that he might bear it after Jesus." - Luke 26:23 (KJV)

According to Roman law, those who were sentenced to crucifixion had to carry their own crosses, but since Jesus had endured so much, there came a point when he was unable to do so any more. That's when the Roman soldiers recruited Simon to carry it until they reached Golgotha; then, Jesus picked up His cross and continued carrying it (John 19:17).

Humility requires us to not only lean on God but to accept the assistance of other willing believers. It sometimes places us in a position where we have to ask for help, and we'll have to endure. Jesus had been beaten, spit on, mocked, and accused. The core of who He was had been disrespected. The crown of thorns placed on His head was a mockery of His kingship and identity. They really pressed Jesus on every side.

The Bible says that Jesus despised the shame yet endured the cross because of the joy set before Him. Jesus had something to look forward to that included us, as believers, coming into fellowship with Him and His father.

After Jesus endured the cross and was resurrected, we see Him praying prior to His ascension into heaven:

"Neither pray I for these alone, but for them also which shall believe on me through their word;

That they all may be one; as thou, Father, art in me, and I in thee, that they also may be one in us: that the world may believe that thou hast sent me." John 17:20-21 (KJV)

"O righteous Father, the world hath not known thee: but I have known thee, and these have known that thou hast sent me.

And I have declared unto them thy name, and will declare it: that the love wherewith thou hast loved me may be in them, and I in them." - John 17:25-26 (KJV)

Jesus had completed the work, or purpose, for which He was made manifest: to reveal the Father, destroy the works of Satan on Earth, and to bring mankind back into fellowship with God.

Jesus also showed that after brokenness has been endured properly, there will be promotion.

Jesus was able to be in a place of rest and assurance, even while going through His brokenness, because He knew it was God's will. Because that fellowship had been held so strongly, Jesus knew He was walking in God's purpose and will, so He was willing to endure.

After His process, Jesus was elevated back to His place as the Son of God. He was exalted to His place of glory so everyone could see who He is.

During the process of His brokenness, Jesus' position as King was mocked. His very identity as the Son of God, and His power and authority to deliver, was ridiculed. However, these are the very areas where His glory was revealed.

Often, the areas where we experience the most opposition are the areas God desires most to show His glory.

Now, thousands of years after Jesus Christ —God in the flesh lived, died , and rose again, He is still being glorified all over the world. In fact, there's no other name under heaven by which men can be saved, and at Jesus' name, every knee must bow and tongue confess that Jesus is, indeed, Lord.

According to Jesus' example, we can expect glory after we have endured our cross. In Romans, the question is asked, 'How can we reign with Him if we have not suffered with Him?' There's a greater purpose in suffering with Christ that will end in promotion and glory.

> *"And if children, then heirs; heirs of God, and joint-heirs with Christ; if so be that we suffer with him, that we may be also glorified together." - Romans 8:17 (KJV)*

> *"If we suffer, we shall also reign with him: if we deny him, he also will deny us:" - 2 Timothy 2:12 (KJV)*

If you're one who's been operating according to your own will instead of Christ's, that means you have been acting like the first Adam. When we operate from the Spirit, we're acting like Jesus Christ, the last Adam. Many times, God will allow brokenness in our lives to bring us back to Jesus Christ. Fellowshipping with Christ, through suffering, can bring us to repentance. In the Greek, "repent" means "to have a change of mind or simply change." Our thinking is changed from going in the wrong way to going in God's way through Jesus Christ and God's Word. So, God is good, even in His allowance of brokenness. This is why we have to give thanks in all things; because all things are always working together for our good.

Definition of repentance in Greek: "a change of mind, as it appears to one who repents, of a purpose he has formed or of something he has done." - Thayer Definition

"Or do you despise the riches of His goodness, forbearance, and longsuffering, not knowing that the **goodness of God leads you to repentance***?" - Romans 2:4 (KJV)*

"That I may know him, and the power of his resurrection, and the fellowship of his sufferings, being made conformable unto his death;" - Philippians 3:10

When we're tempted to doubt or when we become overwhelmed by our circumstances, we should look at Jesus. This will help us remember how things will turn out for us.

We are here to represent Christ on Earth, and in doing so, we represent the Father.

Chapter 16

Nuggets

Nugget #1: Your weaknesses are simply an opportunity for God to work. Remember, His strength is made perfect in our weakness.

Nugget # 2: Be thankful for your family, regardless of the rough patches you've been through. Your family trains you to handle life, whether the experience seemed good or bad. I've learned more from my parent's imperfections than their strong suits.

Nugget # 3: Sometimes, letting go makes room for better.

Nugget # 4: Humility precedes promotion.

Nugget # 5: Often, shaky times that come out of the blue, signal transition. These times are letting you know that heaven; has a place for you to go, and Heaven is stretching your faith to bring your faith to where Heaven is taking you.

Nugget # 6: Complaining will leave you stuck, while thankfulness sets the runway for you to take flight.

Nugget # 7: Sometimes, God will part the Red Sea; other times, He'll require you to walk on water, trusting Him to hold you up.

Nugget # 8: Remember it is God's will for you to be whole, so don't settle in believing you should be broken. And you are whole in him, who is the head of all principality and power. - Colossians 2:10 (KJV)

Nugget # 9: We are at our greatest rest when we are fully trusting in God.

Nugget # 10: My faith is the battering ram that knocks open the door to what I am believing God for.

Nugget # 11: You won't have rest if you don't have faith; and you won't have faith without building yourself up in the Word of God.

Nugget # 12: What is the Lord saying to you? If you know what everyone else is saying but not what God is saying, something is wrong.

Nugget # 13: Don't be in a hurry to be in a relationship. Do be in a hurry to please God.

Nugget # 14: Your worth doesn't come from your relationship status. Your worth comes from God.

Nugget # 15: Believe that you're worthy, even when others tell you that you're not.

Nugget # 16: Always stay in peace, and always have hope.

Nugget # 17: Don't allow what transpires in your life to make you bitter; instead, allow it to make you better.

Nugget # 18: Bitterness leaves us stuck, while forgiveness keeps us growing and moving forward.

Nugget # 19: Walking through many trials and tribulations, one after the other, doesn't mean we're doing something wrong. Sometimes, it means we're doing something right.

"Yes, and all that will live godly in Christ Jesus shall suffer persecution. But evil men and seducers shall wax worse and worse, deceiving, and being deceived. But continue thou in the things which thou hast learned and hast been assured of, knowing of whom thou hast learned them; And that from a child thou hast known the holy scriptures, which are able to make thee wise unto salvation through faith which is in Christ Jesus." - 2 Timothy 3:12-15 (KJV)

Nugget # 20: People tend to believe what they build their faith toward. So, keep building your faith toward God's word, and avoid negative thinking and speaking that opposes His Word.

Nugget # 21: Keep your tongue in line with what God has said. Keep your mouth closed when you don't feel like speaking in line with what God has said.

Nugget # 22: Don't forget that you still have power to decree a thing. It will happen as long as your decree is in line with God's Word and timing for your life.

After going through many disappointments, we may lose the boldness to decree a thing, forgetting who we are in Christ, but being able to decree still belongs to God's sons and daughters. Just be willing to submit to God if He says, "No," "not yet," or "I have something better." God likes to do more, and He loves to exceed our expectations. Sometimes, our thinking is too small concerning what we've decreed, and God has to let it ride.

"You will also decree a thing, and it shall be established unto thee: and the light shall shine upon thy ways". - Job 22:28 (KJV)

"You can make many plans, but the LORD's purpose will prevail." - Proverbs 19:11 (NLT)

"Commit thy way unto the LORD; trust also in him; and he shall bring it to pass." - Psalms 37:5 (KJV)

Nugget # 23: You gotta take your eyes off of other people. Where you are going is not where everyone else will go. Your purpose is unique to you as your training from God will be unique to you as well. You cannot compare what you are required to go through to what others are allowed to avoid.

"We do not dare to classify or compare ourselves with some who commend themselves. When they measure themselves by themselves and compare themselves with themselves, they are not wise." - 2 Corinthians 10:12 (NIV)

Nugget # 24: You can get past the hard places in life.

Nugget # 25: Keep moving forward when it feels like you have no choice but to give up. Your morning will come.

"Weeping may endure for a night, but joy cometh in the morning." - Psalms 30:5 (KJV)

Supplements

God is Jehovah Rapha, The Lord Our God who Heals Us

There's a place in scripture where God describes himself as "Jehovah Rapha," The Lord our God who heals us. This title is mentioned in a story where the children of Israel had come out of Egypt. They'd been journeying in the wilderness for three days, so they were thirsty. However, they couldn't find any water. Without their thirst being quenched, they would have became ill and died.

Then, Israel got their hopes up when they came upon a spring called Marah. Finally, they'd found water. Unfortunately, they couldn't drink it because the water was bitter. Marah means bitter.

Sometimes, life will present things that seem life-giving. They appear to be good for us, yet when we try them, we're disappointed because what we'd hoped would sustain us was bitter, so bitter, that our hope remained delayed.

The Bible says that God brought Israel to this point to prove them, meaning to challenge and prepare them to continue depending on Him as He (God) alone is shown as their provider. So, God had Moses grab a stick and throw it in the water. After this act, the bitterness was removed from the spring, and the water became sweet and safe to drink.

God wanted Israel to know that He is the God of the impossible. He is the one who makes the bitter places in life sweet. He is Jehovah Rapha, The Lord our God who heals us. Whatever we face in life, we know that God is able to heal us, and He will when we look to Him.

Finally, God made a decree with Israel after this incident. "He said," 'If you listen carefully to the voice of the LORD your God and do what is right in his eyes, if you pay attention to his commands and keep all his decrees, I will not bring on you any of the diseases I brought on the Egyptians, for I am the Lord, who heals you (Exodus 15:26)."

That final word is lasting encouragement to those who've been broken while doing what's right before the Lord and seeing no fruit. It's a reminder to continue relying on the Lord, even when it appears contradictory. The Lord, Jehovah Rapha, will come through, doing the miraculous and healing us at the same time. Be encouraged to live a life of wholeness.

An Ungodly Soul-tie's Sole Purpose is to Get You Stuck

An ungodly soul tie's sole purpose is to get you stuck. That means stuck in unrealized potential, wasted time, and lack of peace. An ungodly soul-tie is normally an unequally yoked relationship. This means a relationship tied together by unlawful means a.k.a. both parties are not walking in the same direction that God has set forth in each of their lives. Thus, an ungodly soul-tied relationship cannot have peace. It will be an emotional roller coaster for no reason at all other than it being a mismatched relationship. Why would anyone want to be tied in this type of relationship? Well, we have a choice. We can choose to be bound, or we can choose to be free. A wise person once said, "How can God give us His promise if we have something else in place where God's promise would go?" Those who hold on to ungodly soul-tied relationships are not living in faith; they're accepting what is readily available. Whatever is not of faith is sin. The only thing that should be in the space of God's promise is faith. Our faith allows us to receive it. The person who feels their only choice is to settle for a relationship based on an ungodly soul tie needs to remind himself of who he is by looking into the mirror of God's Word. Deception and double-mindedness are the products of an ungodly soul-tied relationship, which is why a person in this type of relationship needs to be reminded of who he is. (Read James 1:22-25)

In this situation, there's a great need for self-love and allowing one's-self to be built up in God's word. There also needs to be godly accountability to keep encouraged. It's not God's will for us to be stuck. If you find yourself in the same cycles again and again, in a dead-end relationship that is clearly an ungodly soul-tie, start breaking free today!

Brokenness Doesn't Always Mean Weakness

When you see me broken, it doesn't mean I am weak. In fact, that's when I am at my strongest because that's when I am closest to God. That is when I am at a moment where I have nothing, but to depend on God. His strength is made perfect in weakness. He is near to those with a broken and contrite heart. He will not despise. Instead of wondering what I did wrong, or trying to figure me out, pray that I'll have the strength to endure the process as God prepares to elevate me.

Yes, many of God's people have been through seasons of brokenness because of the elevation required in their next season. Let's not forget that the Word says to let the brother of low degree rejoice in that he will be exalted, but the person who is full and rich rejoice because he will be humbled. This is a process that the Lord allows for the believer so that we'll see our own futility and our core need for Jesus Christ. Praise God for brokenness allowed and/or orchestrated by God, because that brokenness is actually for our good!

The Struggle of A Woman

I was a girl with a dream to one day have someone who loved and wanted me. I wasn't picky knowing that I am beautiful just not the most beautiful or the most sought after. I felt I had to choose from my choices a small to non existent pool. I quickly learned that no one at all would be better than the choices I saw. So, I hid myself under the Lord along with my desires that were God-given for love. I could not allow them to come to the surface any more unless it was for some one I thought worthy of me. Every now and then, I would peek at the options and choices around me. As others became blessed, I rejoiced for my friends as I told myself that's not for me. Rejection had accidentally become a part of my identity. I hid myself in the Lord again with all of my desires God-given. As a woman, there is a part of me that wants to be free. She wants to be soft, open, safe, and love deep under the covering of a man. I want to hold his hand and be everything he could ever desire in a woman the way God created me to be, but I hid that part of myself in the Lord as I learned to be strong—to do things on my own. I even learned to cover myself, in a sense, to the point where, I stopped expecting someone appropriate. It was the end of my dream hidden in the Lord with a few other things covering me, like I don't need a man to save me. Real love is for people like her not me. Maybe, one day someone will want me. I hide. The best thing that I know how to do is hide. This has been my life. God started to put his finger on my additional covering of rejection telling me he never gave that to me, but an overflow of his love, an ability to display his power boldly, and that with a sound mind of peace. All fear of rejection had to go at God's command. I look back now and think about all the times God told me to take heart over and over again through this process. God was exchanging my perspective of me for how he sees me, and how he made me before the world was. He pre-ordained me and claimed me as his own. It was the hardest process to get over, but today I am free. No more chains of rejection and not feeling good enough are binding me. I know I am not the prettiest, but I am who I am, and have to accept me, so I do. I'm still hidden longing one day to be free to love and express myself in ways that I have not been able to before under the covering of a godly man who is mature, young, and strong. I scan with my eyes, yet most certainly pray with my heart asking the Lord when will it be safe to allow a guy in. At the Lord's silence, I hide myself again not even paying attention. Lord, awake me when it's safe. The woman's struggle is to love and accept herself in the absence of a man. We as women so easily get our identity from the man and if inappropriate men are around we have inappropriate worth and do inappropriate things below our worth. It's like a curse that we have to come up from under and find our identity in Christ. The Lord is slowly rebuilding the image of how I see myself in Him more content than ever—ready to fly. In Christ there is a freedom that comes with the newness of life. This freedom causes me to be bold, confident, and embracing of myself for who I am, God's beautiful work of art on display for his glory, and being made with the brush of grace and love. I'm more content than I've ever been knowing that the greatest and brightest part of my beauty comes from within—clothed in God's righteousness, holiness, love, kindness, and grace. This beauty that defines me can never be taken away. I stand among many of God's precious and brightest jewels. Seeing myself as beautiful on the outside as well as within.

That's who we are God's mighty and precious jewels and that makes us all beautiful as women despite our struggles.

For more wisdom and encouragement on life lessons, please visit and follow my blog, Intercession For A Generation, on all social media websites. I write a weekly blog discussing life & relationship lessons from a Biblically-sound perspective. Thank you, once again, for reading my book. Additionally, see the action plans at the end of this book, and you may order my first book, "The Single Christian Woman's Guide," on my blog . God bless you all!

Book Information/Social Media Information		
"The Single Christian Woman's Guide": *Wisdom in Getting to Our God Ordained Man of Promise* www.intercession4ageneration.org Available at all major online retailers	[Facebook]	Intercession For A Generation
	[Instagram]	@intercession4ag
	[Twitter]	@intercession4ag
	[YouTube]	Intercession For A Generation
	BLOG - Life & Relationship Lessons	www.intercession4ageneration.org

WHOLENESS ACTION PLAN HANDOUT:

☐ Prioritize Seeking the Lord

This includes intentional prayer, reading the Word, plus listening to what the Lord gives you during your quiet time. Often, it will be a scripture He wants you to look into and meditate on; He'll show you more as you read the specific verse(s) and surrounding scriptures. Also, remember to journal, writing down anything you feel the Lord gives you. You may need to look at it again in the future.

Matthew 6:33 - *But seek ye first the kingdom of God, and his righteousness; and all these things shall be added unto you." (KJV)*

In short, the more that we begin to prioritize God in our lives, the more things will fall in line. This doesn't mean life will always be easy, but everything will always be okay.

☐ Forgive Anyone That You Need To

Unforgiveness hinders us in so many ways. It prevents us from receiving forgiveness from God; it opens the door to a tormenting spirit; unforgiveness distracts our intimacy with God; and it causes us to become stuck. Do yourself a favor, and decide to forgive anyone who's wronged you in any way, including yourself. Ask God to give you the strength to forgive and to show you anyone you may need to forgive. Many times, we don't even realize we need to forgive certain people. Here's something to consider: When we need to forgive someone, we usually think about him/her a lot, we feel negatively or have ill will toward him/her, or we avoid him/her altogether. Allow the Lord to break any unforgiveness in your life.

☐ Be Intentional About Placing Yourself Within Godly Accountability

This can include life groups, small groups at church, or one that you start yourself for like-minded individuals. Be intentional about making godly friends who will push you toward Christ. Also, for the ladies, look into Pinky Promise, a women's group through Heather Lindsey's website. Visit www.pinkypromise.com to find a local group. Heather's husband also has a group for men called The Man Cave and a yearly conference. Visit www.themancaveconference.com to look them up on social media.

Additionally, visit www.meetup.com to look for Christian small groups or groups of interest where you can find accountability and meet like-minded individuals. (There's a possibility that as Intercession For A Generation grows, I'll open up small groups once again).

To be a whole and successful Christian person, you must have accountability. It will challenge and cause us to grow in ways we didn't know we could.

☐ Pursue Your Purpose

The closer you get to God, the more intense your passion will be for what He created you to do, whether it's writing movies or books, speaking, or teaching. Look for opportunities to volunteer and connect with those in your field of study. For example, if your passion is film, look into a local Film Office for your city. Or, research opportunities to volunteer as a P.A. (production assistant). Now is the time to become skillful in your passions and God-given purpose.

Volunteering is one of the best ways to give birth to and sharpen our skills. We feel less pressure when we're simply volunteering instead of doing it for a paycheck; if we get fired, we haven't lost anything. Instead, we've gained valuable experience that shape us into extraordinary people because we stepped out on faith and volunteered. Many of our great singers began in the church. Church often provides a safe place for us to learn and develop in our God-given gifts through volunteering.

☐ Aim to Think Positively

"We demolish arguments and every pretension that sets itself up against the knowledge of God, and we take captive every thought to make it obedient to Christ." – 2 Corinthians 10:5 (NIV)

This scripture speaks about the opposition against our knowledge of God and what He's said concerning us. This opposition is to be expected even from church people, and our response should be to arrest every negative or contrary thought, making it obedient to Christ.

Replace every negative thought with a scripture from God's Word. For example, if you have the thought, 'I'm not good enough to have God's best,' replace it with: God came to give me life and that more abundantly.' (John 10:10) 'God has His best for me.'

☐ Intend to Love Yourself

You'll face a lot of things that can distract you from loving yourself. It could be people misunderstanding you; an inbalance in your schedule. causing you to give too much of yourself; impatience, or an unhealthy relationship. Whatever the reason, be intentional about loving yourself.

Loving you starts with:

- Loving God with all of you
- Loving Yourself
- And then loving others

"'Teacher, which is the greatest commandment in the Law?'

Jesus replied: "'Love the Lord your God with all your heart and with all your soul and with all your mind.' This is the first and greatest commandment. And the second is like it: 'Love your neighbor as yourself.' All the Law and the Prophets hang on these two commandments. Matthew 22:36-40 (NIV)

The flow of your outreach and your relationships should happen only in this manner. God shows us how valuable we are in how He consistently treats us. When we begin treating ourselves in the same manner, our love for others flows from this.

On a separate sheet of paper, make a list of things that you can do regularly to show love to yourself. Begin doing the things you've written down on the list.

☐ Enjoy Life

Despite how circumstances can get us down, it's God's will for us to have joy, and it's His joy that gives us strength.

"Nehemiah said, "Go and enjoy choice food and sweet drinks, and send some to those who have nothing prepared. This day is holy to our Lord. Do not grieve, for the joy of the Lord is your strength." – Nehemiah 8:10 (NIV)

This command for the children of Israel to enjoy themselves was given after they'd been in captivity for several years in Babylon and now lived under King Cyrus. God touched Nehemiah's heart to rebuild the wall of Jerusalem and to celebrate his people's return to their land of promise that God vowed to Abraham, Moses, and the Israelites through the prophet, Jeremiah.

Our joy comes from abiding in Christ, and through that, other things that increase our joy expands; so we have to intend to have joy. We must have faith when things don't seem joyful. We have to know that joy belongs to us, God's children, and it is, indeed, His will. He takes pleasure in seeing us full of joy.

If ye keep my commandments, ye shall abide in my love; even as I have kept my Father's commandments, and abide in his love. **These things have I spoken unto you, that my joy might remain in you, and that your joy might be full.**" *John 15:10-11 (KJV)*

Begin doing things you like to do or try something new so you can enjoy life. You can search sites like Groupon and LivingSocial for special discounts on certain activities. If you like fitness, for example, search for that. If you like trying food from various cultures, search food tasting events in your city.

☐ Speak God's Word over Yourself & Affirm Yourself

We have to be very careful what we say because our words determine what we get and can hinder what God actually has for us. Make sure that what you say is in line with God's

Word for your life. If it's not in agreement, simply don't say it. Go back to 2 Corinthians 10:5, and figure out which scripture to meditate on to renew your mind in that area.

Also, increase your intimacy with God. It is through spending intimate time with Him that we understand His will for our lives. True intimacy with God is a lifestyle of worship. It is obeying Him even when it doesn't feel good. We do this through faith because our faith pleases God. Our worship is stirred, and He shows us His will and purpose for us, changing our minds from our old way of thinking. When God renews our minds, and we see more clearly how He feels about us, we'll agree with what He says and speak that over ourselves.

"Therefore, I urge you, brothers and sisters, in view of God's mercy, to offer your bodies as a **living sacrifice, holy and pleasing to God**—*this is your true and* **proper worship***. Do not conform to the pattern of this world, but* **be transformed by the renewing of your mind***. Then you will be able to test and approve what God's will is—his good, pleasing and perfect will." - Romans 12:1-2 (NIV)*

We can re-affirm ourselves with God's Word when it feels like life is against us; then, we can remind ourselves that God is still for us and that His plans are good. *(Jeremiah 29:11)*

In increasing our intimacy with the Lord; it is great to set a specified time to meet with him. This time will assist in keeping us accountable or consistent. It should not be used as a tool to feel condemned however if we miss a particular time or day.

Agreement

I agree to set aside the specified times below to intentionally meet w/God to carry on my intimate relationship with him. (Specify times below; for example, M-F 6 a.m. – 7 a.m., Prayer, Bible Reading, and Quiet Time):

Your time, Monday-Friday _____

Weekend: _____

**Note: This doesn't mean you can't seek the Lord outside of your specified time. We should always be open to communicating w/God, and after a while, it should become natural.

Will You Commit to Follow the Action Plan?

I _____ make a commitment to myself to live a whole life by following the action plan and I will be diligent in walking out what it says.

    Signature _____ Date: _____

You'll notice your life getting brighter and better as the time goes by. You'll also become more aware of God's goodness and more thankful for every step of the path He's placed you on.

"But the path of the just is **as the shining light, that shineth more and more unto the perfect day."** *– Proverbs 4:18* (KJV)

Introduction to the Abbreviated Wholeness Action Plan For Relationships

There are men who specifically prey on women who are broken. They do this because they know that she is often more open to all sorts of sexual exploits.

The broken woman generally lives in a place where she doesn't feel and can't express joy, give or receive love. She simply exists in a cold, dark, and often isolated place. The men who prey on her love that she doesn't care because she's prime game for sex without responsibility.

How can the broken woman hold a man responsible for treating her correctly when she's not treating herself correctly? The low behavior a woman subjects herself to during this time only confirms her dire need for an intervention of some kind to live life from a different perspective.

It's possible to be a broken woman and not put up with inappropriate behavior. In my more recent experience of brokenness, I was able to still maintain a state of sobriety. Yes, I was broken, I was insecure, and life had beaten me down, but someway, somehow, I'd entrusted my brokenness to the Lord. In doing so, I found a place to hide and rest despite how I felt.

At the time, some of my friends were in town, and we'd all gone bowling. Afterward, we prayed together in the van. God used my friends to give me strength when I felt I had none. He will always provide a way to escape every temptation if we include Him in everything.

Some men are offended when they see you're broken, yet not willing to do whatever they suggest. They'll discard you like you're worth nothing to them. Of course, this can temporarily break a woman more, and this was my experience. My response, however, was, 'So what? I'm already broken. I just have to get over this additional brokenness and be thankful that it didn't end up worse.'

I know women who've done things they swore they'd never do, such as sleep with a married man settling for being the side chick. I've known broken women, who gave in to every sexual fantasy with randoms, knowing it wasn't real love, and put up with all types of physical and verbal abuse.

Ladies, when we don't give our brokenness to God and have godly accountability, but instead give it to sinful sexual and abusive relationships, we're continuing the cycle of brokenness. I call this a cycle because we repeat these situations and these types of men because we think that's all we're worth.

I'm so glad that the truth is our worth as God's daughters and sons is consistent no matter what state of life we're in. That's the beauty of the prodigal son's story. There was not enough work he could do for his father to accept him.

After the prodigal son screwed up, he assumed he would no longer be accepted by his father. He saw himself being lower than a servant in his father's house. His conclusion was that he'd go back home and work to gain his father's approval and at least have the basic necessities.

However, his father quickly debunked that "lower than, not good enough" attitude , that "I had my chance and blew it" mentality. To disprove that wrong thinking, the father quickly gathered the best items in his house that represented royalty. The royal robe, ring, and the sandals were placed upon the prodigal son so he could see himself for who he really was, apart from his experience of brokenness.

This is how God saw him, and this is the Father's heart toward us. God's heart is consistent, no matter what we've gotten ourselves involved in; His love, care, and identity for us remains the same. There's nothing we can do to change it; we are fully accepted and loved in Christ.

God will go beyond the norm to remind us how He feels about us. A guy broke up with me who probably felt that he'd be able to go further with me physically than I allowed. He was disappointed with my standard and the fact that I held to it. Because I was broken while also dealing with some serious family issues, perhaps he thought being physical would be an outlet for me, but it wasn't.

He let me go as if I had absolutely no worth despite thinking he might be different and not drop me because of my values. He no longer wanted to pursue me nor fight for our relationship. As a matter of fact, I saw it crumbling way before it did, and I was the only one willing to try to make it work.

Well, the night we had our final conversation, I literally felt the arms of God around me, holding me throughout the night. I felt such peace and rest even though I should have been sad; I guess God wanted me to get a good night's sleep. In the morning, fear tried to creep up preety hard. It was the fear of being alone because my standard was too high.

I had to deal with that fear by constantly meditating on God's Word. I kept telling myself, God had not given me the spirit of fear, but love, power, and a sound mind. In that case, I needed the power to continue to stay in agreement with what God said about me versus how I was being treated. I had to continue to believe I was worth more when men and others said I was worth less.

The thought of God loving me enough to go beyond the norm and re-affirm His love for me by holding me all through the night was amazing. God saw, and He cared. He is truly near to those that are of a broken and a contrite spirit and he will not despise us (Psalms 34:18).

I want to encourage you to remember that in spite of how broken you feel, you are whole in Christ.

> "So you also are complete through your union with Christ, who is the head over every ruler and authority." - Colossians 2:10 (NLT)

Nothing can separate us from God's love or change the way that He loves us.

For I am persuaded, that neither death, nor life, nor angels, nor principalities, nor powers, nor things present, nor things to come,

Nor height, nor depth, nor any other creature, shall be able to separate us from the love of God, which is in Christ Jesus our Lord." - Romans 8:38-39 (KJV)

The abbreviated wholeness action plan to recover from broken relationships is below:

Abbreviated Wholeness Plan For Relationships

1. Come to an agreement with the brother/sister that you will no longer be talking with them.

You need to be clear that you're discontinuing the relationship. If this has already been done, or you've already been dumped, proceed to step 2. If a relationship is unsafe to have any further communication with the partner; then avoid this step, and move on to step 2.

2. Delete the number from your phone and block or unfollow the person on social media.

Once the door has been closed, it's important not to leave any trails back to that same door. Delete the phone number, and all text message threads. Don't give yourself a way back into that relationship. Get rid of pictures, music, movies, and gifts, or put them away until you're strong enough to get rid of them or they no longer hold value to you. Be honest with yourself on this. No Facebook stocking. Hit the block.

3. Set boundaries.

If you have children or mutual friends with the ex, you won't be able to avoid them completely. In these cases, you'll need some boundaries when dealing with them. Maybe, for example, you won't have them in your home when picking up the children unless someone else is there. Only you know what boundaries you need to set. Again, be honest with yourself. You may also want to have your accountability partner hold you to your boundaries by checking in with you. Additionally, seek wisdom from other single parents who've overcome in this area.

4. Identify what led you to the broken relationship, and deal with that issue.

Often, rejection and insecurity are the culprits that cause us to commit to broken relationships. We may believe we're not good enough for anything else, or we may not realize there's better out there. Be intentional about identifying healthy relationships, and set practical steps to do so. Build up your network of healthy friends, family, associates, and most importantly a healthy view of yourself. If a healthy relationship with the opposite sex is not available right now; simply wait for it while you focus on other things. Don't force yourself into a relationship before you are ready or before an appropriate time.

5. Follow the remaining steps in the previous action plan.

6. Ask yourself what you really want.

If you start to question whether you should continue on the path to wholeness, ask yourself what do you want? Do you want more of the same? Or do you want better? If your answer is better, be willing to do what's necessary to get better.

If you're sexually active and single, commit to stop having sex. Working through the following questions can assist you in doing so:

What were some of the triggers that caused me to become sexually active?

Was I using sex to feel wanted or loved?

What are some healthy things I can do to remind myself I am loved?

What are some things I can do to replace my response to those triggers to avoid being sexually active?

What boundaries can I set in my personal life to avoid sex?

How will avoiding sex before marriage benefit me? (Without an understanding of why you're doing what you're doing (in this case, becoming celibate), you will not continue to do it.) The Bible says that without a vision, the people perish. You need an understanding of where you're going to do what's necessary to get there.

Are you trying to achieve peace of mind? Stop having sex!

Are you trying to produce greater clarity in your discernment? Stop having sex!

Are you trying to avoid STDs and unplanned pregnancy? Stop having sex!

Are you trying to break free from emotional soul-ties? Stop having sex!

Are you trying to re-gain self-control? Stop having sex!

Do you have a desire to experience genuine intimacy that encompasses more than just physical intimacy? Stop having sex!

List Further Personal Notes:

Counseling Resources:

National Sexual Assault Hotline: This national hotline, operated by RAINN (Rape, Abuse & Incest National Network), serves people affected by sexual violence. It automatically routes the caller to their nearest sexual assault service provider. You can also search your local center here or call **800.656.HOPE**

National Domestic Violence Hotline: Through this hotline, an advocate can provide local, direct service resources (safehouse shelters, transportation, casework assistance) and crisis intervention. Interpreter services are available in 170 languages, and they also partner with the Abused Deaf Women's Advocacy Center to provide a videophone option. Hotline number: **800.799.SAFE**

Malesurvivor.org: This site has information and a therapist search for male survivors of sexual violence.

National Suicide Prevention Lifeline provides crisis suicide intervention, self-harm counseling and assistance, and local mental health referrals. Calls are routed to local centers. Hotline: **800.273.TALK (8255)**; for the **Spanish line,** call **888.628.9454**, and for **TTY: 800.799.4TTY (4889)**